Thomas Boyd

SERIES ON OHIO HISTORY AND CULTURE

George W. Knepper, *Summit's Glory*
Leonard Sweet, *Strong in the Broken Places*
John H. White and Robert J. White Sr., *The Island Queen*
H. Roger Grant, *Ohio's Railway Age in Postcards*
Frances McGovern, *Written on the Hills: The Making of the Akron Landscape*
Keith McClellan, *The Sunday Game: At the Dawn of Professional Football*
Steve Love and David Giffels, *Wheels of Fortune: The Story of Rubber in Akron*
Alfred Winslow Jones and Daniel Nelson, *Life, Liberty, and Property: A Story of Conflict and a Measurement of Conflicting Rights*
David Brendan Hopes, *A Childhood in the Milky Way: Becoming a Poet in Ohio*
John Keim, *Legends by the Lake: The Cleveland Browns at Municipal Stadium*
Richard B. Schwartz, *The Biggest City in America: A Fifties Boyhood in Ohio*
Thomas A. Rumer, *Unearthing the Land: The Story of Ohio's Scioto Marsh*
Steve Love, Ian Adams, and Barney Taxel, *Stan Hywet Hall & Gardens*
William F. Romain, *Mysteries of the Hopewell: Astronomers, Geometers, and Magicians of the Eastern Woodlands*
Dale Topping, edited by Eric Brothers, *When Giants Roamed the Sky: Karl Arnstein and the Rise of Airships from Zeppelin to Goodyear*
Millard F. Rogers Jr., *Rich in Good Works: Mary M. Emery of Cincinnati*
Frances McGovern, *Fun, Cheap, & Easy: My Life in Ohio Politics, 1949–1964*
Larry L. Nelson, editor, *A History of Jonathan Alder: His Captivity and Life with the Indians*
Bruce M. Meyer, *The Once and Future Union: The Rise and Fall of the United Rubber Workers, 1935–1995*
Steve Love and Ian Adams, *The Holden Arboretum*
Joyce Dyer, *Gum-Dipped: A Daughter Remembers Rubber Town*
Melanie Payne, *Champions, Cheaters, and Childhood Dreams: Memories of the Soap Box Derby*
John Flower, *Downstairs, Upstairs: The Changed Spirit and Face of College Life in America*
Wayne Embry and Mary Schmitt Boyer, *The Inside Game: Race, Power, and Politics in the NBA*
Robin Yocum, *Dead Before Deadline: . . . And Other Tales from the Police Beat*
A. Martin Byers, *The Ohio Hopewell Episode: Paradigm Lost and Paradigm Gained*
Edward C. Arn, edited by Jerome Mushkat, *Arn's War: Memoirs of a World War II Infantryman, 1940–1946*
Brian Bruce, *Thomas Boyd: Lost Author of the "Lost Generation"*

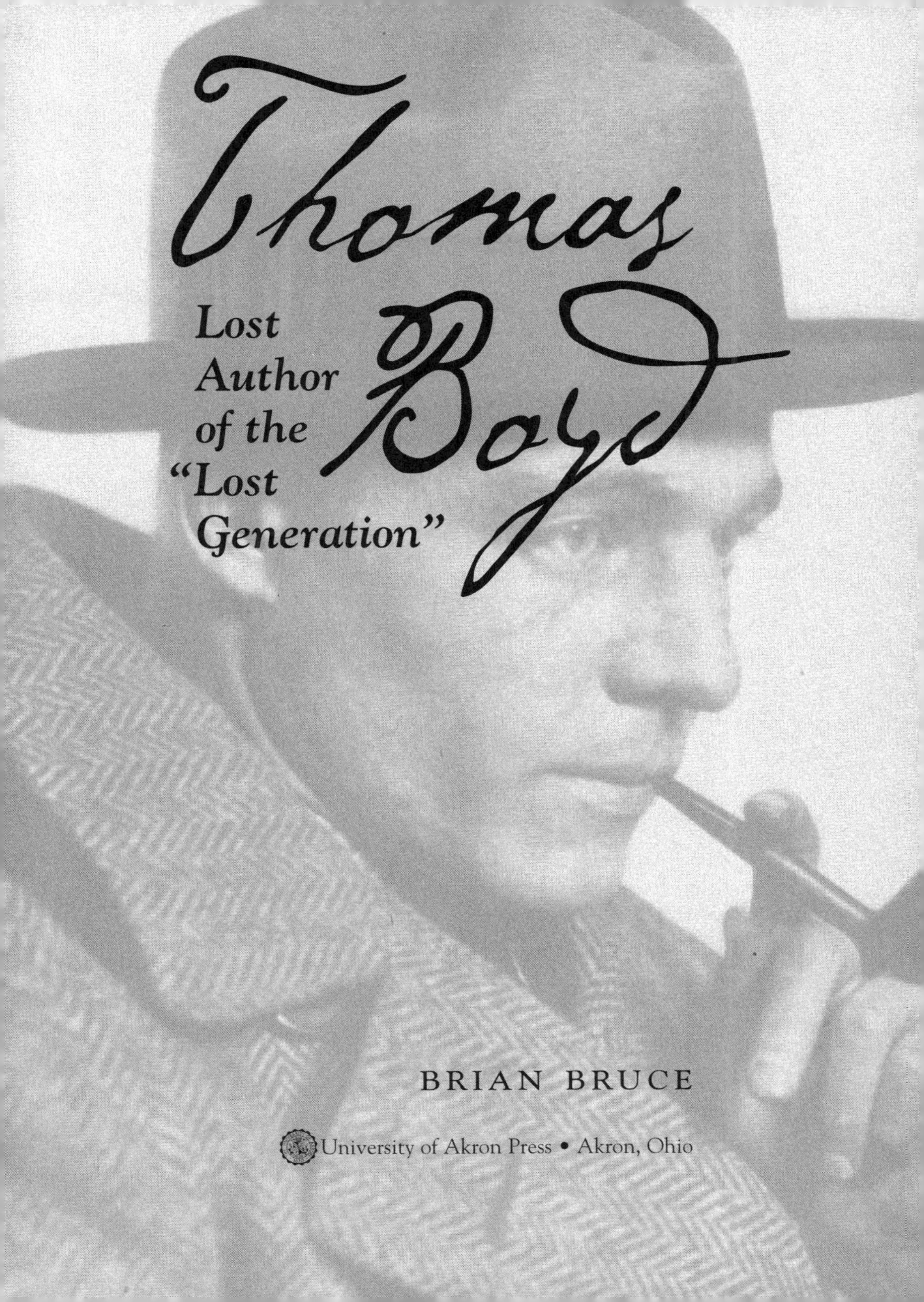

Thomas Boyd

Lost Author of the “Lost Generation”

BRIAN BRUCE

University of Akron Press • Akron, Ohio

First Edition 2006
Manufactured in the United States of America.
10 09 08 07 06 5 4 3 2 1

All inquiries and permission requests should be addressed to the Publisher,
The University of Akron Press, 374B Bierce Library, Akron, Ohio 44325-1703.

Library of Congress Cataloging-in-Publication Data
Bruce, Brian, 1967–
Thomas Boyd : lost author of the lost generation / Brian Bruce.— 1st ed.
p. cm. — (Series on Ohio history and culture)
Includes bibliographical references and index.
ISBN-13: 978-1-931968-33-1 (alk. paper)
ISBN-10: 1-931968-33-0 (alk. paper)
1. Boyd, Thomas, 1898–1935. 2. Authors, American—20th century—Biography. I. Title. II. Series.
PS3503.O9Z55 2006
813'.52—dc22

2006002058

The paper used in this publication meets the minimum requirements of American National Standard for Information Sciences—Permanence of Paper for Printed Library Materials, ANSI z39.48–1984. •

Cover image: Thomas Boyd; courtesy of the Minnesota Historical Society Loc# por 18192 r1 Neg# 75034.

For Terri, Benjamin, and Hannah

contents

acknowledgments

All authors owe debts of gratitude to the people closest to them, to people they know who have helped them directly and indirectly, and to people they may have never met who have nevertheless provided valuable assistance. I am no exception and, in fact, I probably owe more than other authors to other people.

First, this book would not have been possible without the considerable help of Mrs. Elizabeth Boyd Nash. During a correspondence that lasted over several years, she answered numerous questions, offered advice when asked, and generously agreed to trust the U.S. mail with the collection of her father and mother's papers so that I could see and copy them. Unfortunately, Mrs. Nash died before I finished this biography. I can only hope that it would have pleased her.

Dr. Roger Bilstein of the University of Houston Clear Lake served as my faculty advisor while I worked on my master's degree, and I had the honor to be a student in several of his classes. Dr. Bilstein was an excellent teacher and exemplary scholar, and was always generous with his time and expertise. His interest in my work and his encouragement gave me the confidence to continue my research into the life of Thomas Boyd and to pursue publication of this biography. I would also like to thank Dr. Jonathan Zophy of the University of Houston Clear Lake for his excellent teaching and his encouragement.

Several individuals at the libraries and historical societies from whose collections I gathered the material on which this biography is based provided me with the benefit of their knowledge and skills. Thanks are due to Margaret Sherry Rich of the University of Princeton Libraries, Elizabeth

Plummer of the Ohio Historical Society, Dean M. Rogers of Vassar College Libraries, Craig Tenney of Harold Ober Associates, Dennis O. Palmore of New Directions Publishing Corporation, Lydia Zelaya of Simon and Schuster, and special thanks to Brainerd F. Phillipson. I would also like to thank Robert L. Daugherty, editor of *Ohio History;* Anne R. Kaplan and Marilyn Ziebarth, editors of *Minnesota History;* Richard Lingeman; Thomas Boyd Nash; and John Marshall, for the use of his fax machine.

Thanks are also due to Dr. Ann Guess, a friend and colleague who graciously agreed to read my messy manuscript. She offered suggestions and advice that dramatically improved this book. My mother, Sharon Bruce, was brave enough to read this manuscript twice and to twice attempt to teach her hardheaded son proper comma usage. Thanks, Mom. The help of these two brilliant women was invaluable. However, if, despite their best efforts, errors remain, they are the fault of the author alone.

My family, both immediate and extended, helped keep me working on this book and offered more encouragement than I could have wished for. I hope the publication of this book at least partially repays the debts I owe them. Special thanks to my lovely wife, Terri Bruce, for believing in me, encouraging me, and having infinite patience with me. Thanks to my children, Benjamin and Hannah, for understanding when Dad said he had to work, but couldn't exactly explain what he was working on. Thanks again to my mother for instilling in me a love of books and authors and to my father, Victor Bruce Jr., for giving me a love of history. Thanks are also due to the following family members for the enthusiasm and interest they have shown in this project over the past eight years: Victor Bruce Sr. and Sue Bruce, L. B. Smith and Jessie Smith, Roger Schlegel, Connie Schlegel, Irma Schlegel, Grandma Dee Snook, Richard and Linda Krause (thanks for not looking at me like I was crazy twenty years ago when I said I wanted to be a writer), Shelley and Scott Tatum, Erin and Mike Hornbaker, and Anthony and Stephanie Schlegel.

I'd also like to thank my good friend Richard Roseborough for more late-night conversations than I can count, his editorial efforts on both the articles I published about Thomas Boyd, and his continued support.

Finally, I would like to thank Dr. Michael J. Carley and Amy Freels of the University of Akron Press, whose patience, skill, and professionalism made this possible.

introduction

Today the phrase the "lost generation" calls to mind romantic images of Hemingway scribbling in a notebook in a Paris café, Fitzgerald on a drunken spree in New York or the south of France, or the members of the Algonquin Round Table arguing about plays, books, and art over lunch. While many Americans recognize the names of Hemingway and Fitzgerald and may have read one of their books, few people know the name or work of American author Thomas Boyd and fewer still would place him alongside the other, more famous authors of the "lost generation." But of all the American authors of this period, Gertrude Stein's phrase more aptly describes the life of Thomas Boyd than the lives of his more famous contemporaries. No American author's life and work were more affected by World War I and the events of the first third of the twentieth century than Boyd's.

Compared to Boyd, Fitzgerald and Hemingway had all the advantages. Both Hemingway and Fitzgerald were born into middle-class or upper-middle-class homes and had at least one devoted parent and the opportunity to receive a first-class education. Boyd grew up a virtual orphan without his father and separated from his mother, and had a sporadic education. During World War I, Fitzgerald served as an officer in a unit that never left the United States, and Hemingway served as ambulance driver in the Italian army. Boyd joined the Marine Corps and served as a combat infantryman at the battles of Belleau Wood, Soissons, Saint-Mihiel, and Mont Blanc. He was wounded in a gas attack and probably suffered from post-traumatic stress. After the war Fitzgerald and Hemingway pursued their dreams of becoming writers without serious thought or concerns about earning money. Boyd struggled to find work and to find his niche in society while keeping alive his desire to be a writer. Eventually, Boyd gained the confidence to try his hand at being a newspaper reporter, and from there he became a literary editor of a Minnesota newspaper. By the time Boyd sat down to write his first book, Fitzgerald had already published his second. During their careers Fitzgerald and Hemingway received high praise for their writing and innovative approaches to fiction, were paid top dollar for their short stories, and earned substantial royalties from the sale of their books. Of all Boyd's books, only *Through the Wheat*, his autobiographical World War I novel, received broad and universal critical praise and only three of his books sold more than five thousand copies. Fitzgerald's and Hemingway's struggles to sustain literary greatness contributed to their self-destructive behavior. Boyd's fight to get his work into print and to earn a living as a writer led to his decision to embrace communism. While Fitzgerald and Hemingway eventually committed suicide, either by drink or gunshot, Boyd died of a cerebral hemorrhage brought about in part by wounds he suffered during the war. Unlike Fitzgerald and Hemingway, who strove for literary greatness, Boyd entertained few such notions. Boyd wrote for much simpler reasons. He wrote because he liked being a writer. He wrote in order to earn a living. And he wrote because he had stories that he wanted to tell and believed needed to be told.

Boyd never belonged to any school of literature or followed any distinct literary style. If he was a realist it was because realism suited the subject of his books and his personality. If he was a romantic it was because he romanticized people and events from the past that were the subjects of most of his books. His books can be loosely grouped into three categories: autobiographical books, Ohio books, and Marxist propaganda. These three categories represent the things Boyd cared most about: his experiences and those of his family, Ohio and its history, and, at the end of his life, advancing the communist cause. All of his books, regardless of their subject or the category they fit into, are about men placed in trying situations who often emerge dissatisfied and misunderstood. The struggle of the individual against difficult or impossible circumstances is the theme that unified Boyd's work and reflects the way he saw his own life.

And Boyd led a fascinating life. In his thirty-six years, he was an orphan, a military school cadet, a Marine, a recipient of a medal for bravery, a factory worker, a husband, a socialist, a reporter, a literary editor, a father, a friend and protégé of Sinclair Lewis and F. Scott Fitzgerald, a novelist, a biographer, an adulterer, a failed screenwriter, a communist, and a politician. Throughout his life Boyd searched for acceptance, success, and meaning. This quest made him open to the social and cultural movements that changed the United States. In many ways Boyd's own life mirrored those changes.

It is the purpose of this book to preserve a record of Boyd's life and work for those with an interest in the period and in the "lost generation," to provide a new perspective on the world of American letters during the 1920s and 1930s, and to encourage a reexamination of the life and work of one of America's least-known authors.

chapter one

"they made him feel as if he were . . . a limb of Satan"

On July 3, 1898, the United States Navy scored a stunning victory over the Spanish navy at Santiago Bay, Cuba. That victory doomed the garrison of Spanish soldiers in Santiago and guaranteed eventual American victory in the Spanish-American War. By winning the war, the United States established itself as a world power and began taking a greater part in world affairs. On the same day, in a small, green, wood-frame house in the sleepy Ohio town of Defiance, Thomas Alexander Boyd was born. The birth took place without recorded difficulties, but little else about Boyd's youth would be as uncomplicated. For the next fifteen years, he would live as a practical orphan, moving from one town to another and from family member to family member until, finally, on his own he found a true home. His early personal struggles made him restless and uncertain. That restlessness often brought him into the center of the changes that the United States went through during the first third of the twentieth century. His uncertainty and self-doubt affected his personal and professional relationships for the rest of his life.

Given the disparity between his mother's and father's families and the brevity of their marriage, Thomas Boyd's birth was something of a miracle. His father, Thomas Alexander Boyd Sr., known as Alec, came from a wealthy Montreal family, and his mother, Alice Dunbar, from one of the least successful lines of one of western Ohio's oldest families. They met by chance in Chicago in 1892.

According to family legend, the Montreal Boyds descended from the Scottish earl of Kilmarnock, who fled, along with his eldest son, the first Thomas Alexander Boyd, to North America after losing an eighteenth-century dispute. Alec Boyd took the legend, though unconfirmed and even disavowed by some members of the Boyd family, seriously enough to name his first son after himself and the son of the Scottish earl and to tell his wife the story.

The Boyds of Montreal had done well in the pharmaceutical business, and by the early 1800s had secured a place in Montreal society. Unfortunately for Alec Boyd and his brother Walter, the family's money began to run out in the 1890s. Their father decided to expend the remaining family fortune launching his daughters into society in the hopes that a good marriage would save the family position. His sons would have to make their own way in the world, and he advised them to go to America to search for work.

Heeding his advice, Alec and Walter moved to Chicago and went to work in a real estate firm. Alec, a charming young man of slight build, large sympathetic eyes, and delicate good looks, did very well. Walter, a dark-haired bull of a man with a loud voice and violent temperament, found sales much more difficult and quickly settled on the idea of marrying a wealthy widow. He eventually succeeded.

After a few years, Alec could afford the fine suits and natty attire he loved, and he began to think seriously about marriage. His fine features and sharp dress had made him popular with the young ladies of Montreal and helped him in his business, but in Chicago he had no easy means of introducing himself to women. He wanted to marry but could not find a suitable girl. A chance meeting in Chicago's Grant Park changed that situation.

By 1892 Alice Dunbar had become a beautiful woman. Slim-waisted, narrow-hipped, with beautiful red hair and ramrod-straight posture, she gave the appearance of someone of dignity and importance, but she had not always been a regal beauty.

The oldest daughter of a struggling farmer who had nine daughters before his first son, Alice Dunbar seemed destined for the harsh life of an Ohio farmer's wife. Her father, Samuel Dunbar, was the grandson of William Rohn, one of the earliest settlers in western Ohio. Rohn had established a large, successful farm near Defiance, Ohio, on the very spot where General Anthony Wayne encamped prior to the pivotal Battle of Fallen Timbers. Rohn's daughter Mary married Samuel Dunbar Sr., who eventually took possession of the five-hundred-acre farm. Their son Samuel Dunbar Jr. was Alice Dunbar's father and Thomas Boyd's grandfather. In the 1850s Sam Dunbar Jr. bought a large tract of land in the wilderness outside Defiance and cleared the land for a large farm. The farm eventually failed in part because of the lack of sons who could help with the farm work and in part because of risky loans Sam took to buy expensive farming equipment. At sixteen Alice, in order to relieve some of her father's financial burden, went to live with and work for her great-aunt Charity Rohn. Her cousin Grace Woodward, the granddaughter of Charity Rohn, described Alice during this time as a gangly, awkward, rough-handed, cross-eyed girl whose unkempt hair constantly fell in her face as she worked. Grace often encouraged Alice to go to college and escape farm life, and eventually Alice followed her advice. She turned down an offer of marriage from a young successful farmer and instead moved to Chicago, where she began training to become a nurse at the Illinois Nursing Institute.[1] After completing her training, she worked as an assistant to the superintendent of a Chicago hospital and underwent surgery to uncross her eyes. She lived alone, and her salary made it possible for her to afford the fine clothes she desired. Alice enjoyed her position and independence. Her self-confidence grew. During breaks from her work, she often strolled along the lakeshore in Grant Park. It was there that she met Alec Boyd.[2]

Though they met in 1892, Alec and Alice were not engaged until 1896. Reluctant to give up her independence and career as a nurse for the life of a housewife, Alice prolonged their courtship. Alec proposed and Alice finally accepted Alec's proposal during a boating excursion on Lake Michigan during the summer of 1896. They married December 28 that same year.[3]

At first things went well for Alec and Alice Boyd. Alec continued to prosper in real estate and Alice settled into the life of a middle-class Chicago housewife. She looked up her cousin Grace, who lived in Chicago with her husband, Duncan Smith, a local newspaperman, and went to their apartment. Alice's transformation into a beautiful woman surprised and delighted Grace, though Alice's boasts about wealth and Alec's status as a "gentleman" irritated her. The reunion with her cousin proved fortuitous in the months that followed.

Everything changed for Alice and Alec Boyd in the winter of 1897 when Alec contracted pneumonia and was unable to work. They had saved little money, so Alice, though pregnant with their first child, returned to nursing to support them. Their new poverty forced Alice to sell many of the fine clothes she had purchased, and as Alec's illness lingered, he lost his position at the real estate firm. When they could no longer pay the rent on their apartment and as work become increasingly difficult for Alice, the Boyds moved in with Grace and Duncan Smith.

With the approach of spring 1898, Alec Boyd began to recover. Determined to find work and reestablish his independence, he left the apartment on a cold day in March to look for a job. The exposure to the cold weather caused him to relapse, and he died on April 13, 1898. Alice, destitute financially and emotionally, no longer wanted their baby and was unable to make any decisions. She received no direct help from Alec's family, though they eventually arranged a quick and quiet funeral for Alec. Walter Boyd appeared one day at the door of the Smiths' apartment and demanded whatever money Alice had to help pay for the funeral. Prostrate with grief and unwilling to stand up to Walter, Alice would have given him the little money she had if her cousin Grace had not intervened. Grace took the money from Alice and informed Walter that the money would be needed to help care for the unborn child. When Walter threatened to take the money by force, Grace thrust the money inside her blouse and told Walter that if he wanted the money, he knew where he could find it. Unwilling to assault a woman, Walter left without the money. Despite Grace's heroic efforts, the meager amount of money was not enough to cover Alice's expenses. Without a husband or money, she had no one to turn to but her parents.

Alice returned to Defiance and to her parents, who were unsure what to make of their daughter and were equally uncomfortable with her circumstances. The citizens of Defiance reveled in the fall of the uppity Alice and circulated rumors about her baby's legitimacy. In this atmosphere she gave birth to Thomas Alexander Boyd Jr.[4]

After a brief period of recovery, Alice returned to Chicago and her position with the superintendent of the hospital. She had determined to earn enough money to provide her son with a first-class education. Unfortunately, severe headaches (a side effect of her corrective eye surgery) made working long hours painful. To ease her suffering, a doctor at the hospital prescribed morphine for Alice, and over time she became addicted. Her addiction interfered with her work and caused her to lose her job. The next fifteen years of her life were spent in swings between periods of full-blown drug use and periods of recovery. Alice's work and dependency kept her away from her son for most of his childhood. When she gained control of her life, she worked and saved money for Tom's education; but when she relapsed, she could not work enough to afford to keep him in any private school.

Thomas Boyd spent the first eleven years of his life in the home of his grandparents in Defiance. His mother's absence from his life taught him that she was not someone he could rely on and affected his emotional development. Sam and Martha Dunbar did their best to provide for Tom, but they were old and unprepared to meet all the emotional needs of a young boy. They fed, clothed, and sheltered him, but Tom never felt completely accepted. His grandfather's low opinion of Tom's father carried over to Tom, and the grandfather would often predict a dire future for his grandson. Tom compounded his grandfather's fears by being a mischievous boy. When Tom accidentally burned down a neighbor's barn, Sam Dunbar predicted that Tom would end his life at the end of a hangman's rope. The public schools in Defiance provided Tom little relief. His circumstances were widely known to his classmates, who often teased him about his poverty and his status as a virtual orphan. Tom sought refuge in the isolation of the cornfields and forests that surrounded Defiance and spent many hours wandering alone.

Despite his grandfather's low opinion of Tom's character, or perhaps because of it, Sam Dunbar made up his mind to teach his grandson the history of western Ohio and the history of the Dunbar family. He took Tom with him on short trips to neighboring towns, pointing out sites of historical interest and telling Tom stories of General Anthony Wayne and William Rohn. These trips and conversations were the highlight of Tom's life in Defiance, and he grew to love his grandfather. The lessons Sam Dunbar imparted to Tom created in him a true love of the history of Ohio and a deep appreciation for the history of his family. Later both would become the focus of much of Boyd's work as an author.[5]

When he was eleven, Thomas Boyd's mother, having temporarily gained control over her addiction and having saved enough money, enrolled him in the Ohio Military Academy at College Hill near Cincinnati, where she worked as a private nurse. Tom remained at the academy from 1909 until 1911. No record of his performance remains, but he did receive confirmation at the Grace Catholic Church in College Hill on April 26, 1910. The confirmation was somewhat unusual, given the lack of evidence of religious upbringing during his years in Defiance. When his mother's money ran out, Tom returned to Defiance. In the fall of 1911, Alice had again managed to save some money and this time sent Tom to the Porter Military Academy in Charleston, South Carolina. He stayed in the South for one year, but by the autumn of 1912 Tom was back in Defiance and going to public school. Tom spent part of 1913 living with his mother in Cincinnati and attending Woodward High School.[6] At age fifteen he went to live in the home of an aunt and uncle in Chicago, where he worked as a soda jerk in their drugstore. His stay in Chicago was brief. When the drugstore's register came up short of money, his uncle accused him of stealing and Tom, indignant or guilty, set out on foot for the home of some of his father's relatives in Elgin, Illinois.

When he arrived at the home of his aunt Eleanor Wilde and explained who he was, his aunt took him in. For the next three years she raised him as though he were her son. In his aunt's home, which she shared with her daughter Marion, Thomas Boyd found true acceptance and the stability his childhood had been lacking. Not surprisingly, the Wildes wielded a great deal of influence over Tom, and his time with them had a profound impact on his life.

The Wildes were Christian Scientists. In fact, Eleanor Wilde had been a disciple of Mary Baker Eddy and often read to Tom from her book *Science and Health*. The Wildes and Tom's cousin Mark Yarwood, who also lived in Elgin, were prominent members of the local Christian Science Church. Tom quickly became a convert and even served as an usher at church services. The anti–medical treatment stance of Tom's new religion must have irritated his mother, the nurse, and it is possible that his decision to embrace Christian Science was a form of rebellion. In a 1917 letter to his mother, Tom downplayed his commitment to Christian Science: "I gotta hard task mistress believe me. It is no graft trying to please someone who has the C.S. bug as bad and as inconsistently as she [Marion] has. Do you know that I believe I am a little hypocritical at times."[7] Despite this equivocation, Tom's acceptance of the basic tenets of Christian Science stayed with him into adulthood.

In addition to being Christian Scientists, Marion Wilde and Mark Yarwood were also graduates of Oberlin College and lovers of literature. They exposed Tom to what they considered to be great works of literature and tutored him in literature and writing. George Bernard Shaw became Tom's favorite author, and he began to dream of becoming a writer. His letters to his mother from Elgin contain adolescent bursts of florid prose that showed the influence of the nineteenth-century literature that constituted most of his reading. Tom's early attempts at more formal writing ended in frustration, and he destroyed them all shortly after completing them.

In Elgin, Thomas Boyd continued his sporadic education. He enrolled in the local Elgin Academy, but the teachers and the curriculum did not impress him, and he withdrew after a few semesters.[8] For a time he became a full-time pupil of his cousin's, but eventually he enrolled in a local business school, where he began to learn the principles of accounting and shorthand.[9]

His interests outside literature were typical: he played football for Elgin Academy, longed to buy a car, and was fascinated by the young ladies of Elgin. His letters to his mother frankly expressed his interests and detailed his exploits.[10] In 1916 he wrote, "Marie is leaving for Dubuque tomorrow and she will be gone for the rest of the season. She is a very nice girl 'all wool and a yard wide.' I had made up my mind to have a date every night this week."[11] By 1917 Tom's romantic interest centered around an apparently coy girl name De Ette. That year he wrote his mother:

> And the way my best girl acts! Why, it is simply abominable. I have a date with her Saturday afternoon and this evening I have a date with another girl and Sunday night I have a date with the same one. So you see I do not intend to be a bachelor even if De_____ gives me the K.O. Oh yes, I am pretty well fixed. And then it wouldn't be any fun if she threw herself in my arms for you see I would not know what to do with her.[12]

Despite his seeming nonchalance about De Ette, she would remain the object of his affection even after he left Elgin. Eventually, she eluded him and remained one of the great romantic disappointments of his life.

Though his letters were often boastful, Tom's popularity with girls in Elgin was understandable. A picture taken of him during this time shows him dressed in a dark suit, complete with bowtie; He is sitting in a chair, staring straight into the camera. His wavy blond hair is brushed from his high forehead, his unblemished skin glows, his nose is perfectly straight if a little long, his lips are full, and his penetrating eyes convey the message of a young man confident of the effect of his looks.

Tom also made friends with the young men of Elgin. One in particular, Bob Hepburn, became his best friend. When Bob and his stepmother had a fight, Tom invited Bob to move in with him and the Wildes. Bob stayed with the Wildes a short while before moving to Chicago to live with an aunt. Even after his move, Tom and Bob saw one another regularly and even bought a car together. As news of the Great War reached Elgin and filtered into the consciousness of Tom and Bob, they decided that they had to get involved. They attempted to raise the money to outfit themselves with an ambulance and the equipment necessary to join the American ambulance service in France but fell short. Their determination to participate in what they felt would be the great event of their lifetime did not diminish.[13]

When the United States entered the war in April 1917, Thomas Boyd and Bob Hepburn got their chance. Together they made the trip to a United States Marine Corps recruiting office in Chicago and signed up for immediate service.[14] Tom sent a postcard to his mother, who was living in Ottowa, Illinois, and informed her in rather terse language of his enlistment.[15] Back in Elgin, awaiting the day he was to report for transport to Port Royal, South Carolina, he wrote her another letter expressing some apprehension about his upcoming military service.[16] On May 20, already en route for training camp, Tom sent his mother another postcard in which he confidently expressed his plans for a life in the military: "I expect to embrace my trials and tribulations with great fortitude and much reticence thereby favorably impressing my superiors."[17]

Boyd, like most of the men who volunteered for military service in World War I, had no idea just how much "fortitude" he would have to exhibit to live through the war. And he had no idea what an impact the war would have on his life or on the United States of America. The war would be the pivotal experience of Boyd's life, just as it was a pivotal experience for the United States and an entire generation.

chapter two

"The soul of Hicks was numb"

A PORTRAIT OF THOMAS BOYD and his friend Bob Hepburn taken before they shipped off for France shows the two young men standing side by side in full uniform. Bob's right hand rests on Tom's left shoulder and both men hold their broad-brimmed hats at their waists. Bob's face is placid and confident. Tom's face is more animated. His raised eyebrows, wide-open eyes, and jutting chin give him a look of anticipation. Like many of the young American men who volunteered for military service during the Great War, Thomas Boyd and Bob Hepburn looked on the war as a great adventure and on military service as an opportunity to advance. Those ideas may have been ingrained in Tom during his years in military schools, which no doubt fostered a belief in the glory and honor of combat. Boyd had no political motivation for going to war. His letters betray no deep animosity for the Germans nor love of the Allies, and there is no indication that British propaganda had any effect on him. Whatever his motivation for joining the Marine Corps, he learned that glory and honor were largely absent from the battlefields of northern France. What had seemed like a great adventure in the safety of the recruiting office was, in reality, a confusing and degrading experience that left deep scars on Thomas Boyd and a whole generation of young men and women.

When the United States declared war on Germany on April 6, 1917, its military, the Marine Corps included, was woefully unprepared. Though Congress as a part of the Defense Act of 1916 had approved the expansion of the corps by more than 4,000 men and 349 officers, the number of men in the marines fell some 1,900 men and 170 officers short of the 1916 maximums at the time of the declaration of war. Most of the recruits of 1916 became a part of the 5th Marine Regiment, which sailed for France a few months after war was declared. The post-declaration enlistees were organized into the 6th Marine Regiment.[1]

Thomas Boyd and Bob Hepburn were among the men who made up the newly formed 6th Regiment. They spent their first days of service at Parris Island (Port Royal, South Carolina). Tom arrived there near the end of May 1917. Standard Marine Corps practice required him to pass a number of examinations before being formally inducted. For Boyd this process took little time. On May 26, shortly after his arrival, he wrote a letter to his mother, and as a postscript added just before he mailed the letter, he wrote in a large excited hand, "I have just taken the oath and am a Marine."[2]

Parris Island tested Boyd's enthusiasm. In another of the numerous letters he wrote to his mother while stationed on the island, he described the conditions at the camp and a typical day:

> I am getting along very well, the food isn't the best, the work isn't the easiest, and the toilet facilities aren't the best but I am getting so that I rather enjoy the rough life. We drill about five hours a day, do police duty some of the time, and the rest of the time do most anything they have for us to do.[3]

Despite the hardships, he did not regret his decision: "I am not sorry that I enlisted. I am rather glad I chose that branch of service known as the U.S.

Marines."[4] Besides receiving an introduction to basic drill, the marines on Parris Island spent considerable time on the rifle range. Boyd had high hopes of qualifying as a sharpshooter but in the end failed to do so, qualifying only a little better than first-class marksman.[5]

When the 6th Regiment moved to the newly acquired marine training facilities at Quantico, Virginia, in early July 1917, Boyd's letters home became infrequent. Whether as a result of his growing confidence, fading homesickness, or the ability to visit his mother while on furlough, he wrote little. His last letter to his aunt Marion Wilde from Quantico contained his projections for his immediate future:

> Anyway we are going to France and we expect to leave between tomorrow and Sunday. We will go to Philadelphia on our way over.
>
> I took the examination for corporal today and as far as I know I passed it very well. I am out of the hand-grenade squad—transferred into the machine gun squad—am captain of two guns. We have all of our winter clothing, entrenching tools, etc. and I expect we'll use them before we see the good old USA again.[6]

He correctly assessed and predicted his situation. He had been transferred to the 75th Company of the 1st Battalion of the 6th Marines. He made corporal on September 18, 1917. And he set sail for France from Philadelphia on board the *USS Henderson* on September 16, 1917.[7]

The 6th Regiment arrived in France on October 6, 1917, and was combined with the 5th Regiment to create the 4th Brigade of the 2nd Division of the American Expeditionary Force. With a combined fighting strength of 280 officers and 9,164 men, the 4th Brigade was larger than the average brigade. The 6th also joined the 5th in the work it had been doing since its arrival several months earlier. For the first months of their tour in France, Tom and the other men of the 6th unloaded ships, constructed barracks, dug latrines, and did guard duty.[8] Like most of his fellow marines, Boyd hated the work details and looked forward to actual combat. In a 1918 letter to his mother, he wrote, "And you know I enlisted to fight and not do guard duty, so don't say you hope I keep away from danger. That sounds slackerish."[9] Through his fictional alter ego, William Hicks, the hero of Boyd's first novel, *Through the Wheat*, Tom recorded an even stronger statement of his feelings about this period: "[H]e was supposed to be a soldier. He had enlisted with at least the tacit understanding that he was one day to fight. . . . But was this action? Was this war? . . . Soldiering with a shovel."[10] In reality, Boyd and the 6th did not have to wait long before being sent to the front lines.

One important event did occur during Boyd's time as a rear-echelon laborer. He was found asleep while on guard duty by, of all people, Bob Hepburn. Bob reported the incident to their commander and Boyd was brought before Major Adams on charges that could have resulted in a court-martial. Adams, who recognized Boyd's value as a soldier, did not court-martial him, but he did "bust him down" to the rank of private. This demotion disappointed Boyd a great deal because he had been scheduled to take the sergeants' exam in a few weeks. Though Bob had been the one to report him, he and Tom remained friends for the duration of the war.[11]

The men of the 6th finally got the opportunity to experience combat in March 1918 when they relieved a French division in the trenches just south of the killing fields of Verdun. These trenches were among the oldest and best maintained on the western front, but they were still damp, uncomfortable, and plagued by lice and rats.[12] From the time Thomas Boyd went into the front lines until he entered an army hospital near the end of the war, he wrote infrequently. The few letters he did write were, understandably, uninformative. He did keep a diary, in which he set down most of his combat experiences and which he used in writing the novel *Through the Wheat*. In the novel he described life in the trenches in unpleasant terms:

> Dawn broke upon a desolate field where rusty barbed wire clung awkwardly to the post on which it had been strung. There were a few gnarled and stunted trees, the wreck of what had once been a French farmhouse, and that was all. Hicks peered over the parapet, wondering how near he was to the enemy . . .

> [T]here lay very heavy on his head a steel helmet that, though he had thought it chic for a while, was now no more distinguished looking than the aluminum dish in which his food was rationed to him. He had worn his drab shirt for two weeks and there were black rings around the collar and wrists. His gas mask, girded over his chest, looked foul and unclean. . . . The knees of his breeches were as soiled and as uncomfortable as his shirt, and his puttees and shoes were crusted with dried mud.[13]

The 6th Regiment's stay in the trenches was not without incident. The men experienced their first barrage of long-range artillery, and the Germans, aware of the presence of the inexperienced Americans opposite them, conducted numerous raids on their position. There were many casualties. One company lost forty men in a single barrage of phosgene gas. On the whole, the 6th suffered—128 killed and 744 wounded—during its month-long stay at the front. The troops had been introduced to the rigors of modern warfare, but nothing could have prepared them for what they would go through in the next five months.

Near the end of June 1918, the 4th Brigade was abruptly withdrawn from a rest area near Montdidier and rushed into position along the Château-Thierry–Paris road in order to stop a German advance that was rolling up the French divisions and threatening Paris itself. Despite their untried status, the marines of the 4th Brigade played a pivotal role in halting the last German push of World War I.[14]

The German assault, which began on May 27 and consisted of fifty divisions, had been carefully planned. The squeaks and rattles of thousands of caissons had been carefully muffled, and the three hundred thousand soldiers hid in forests during the day and traveled at night. When the assault began, it came as a complete surprise to the French troops massed along the Chemins des Dames; they broke and ran toward Paris, leaving behind men and machinery. Although the thrust toward Paris had been intended as a diversion, German General Ludendorf, convinced that victory was within his grasp, changed his strategy and made an all-out push for the French capital.[15] The American 2nd Division, which had originally been scheduled to relieve the American 1st Division at Cantigny, was reluctantly turned over to the French command to help stop the German advance.

The convoy of trucks that carried the 2nd Division into position stretched for miles and wound past thousands of French refugees.[16] Thomas Boyd rode in the back on one of those trucks, and in *Through the Wheat* he describes the scene. As the truck passes a family of refugees who had all their worldly possessions piled on a cart, a marine shouts out, "'Don't you worry, pappy. We'll get your home back for you.' The sentiment was taken up and voiced by a great number. Through the warm glow of the spirit of the crusader it gave them, all other emotions were submerged."[17] That pleasant feeling of confidence would not last.

The question of where to place the 4th Brigade of the 2nd Division in order to help stop the German advance and simultaneously relieve the steadily retreating French Division perplexed the French command, which ultimately allowed the American commanders to make the decision. Near four o'clock on the afternoon of June 1, 1918, the men of the 6th Marines established a defensive line north of the Château-Thierry–Paris road between Lucy and Belleau Wood. Through this position retreated the scattered remains of broken French divisions.[18] Boyd witnessed the retreat:

> From another woods, in front and to the left of the platoon, ran soldiers in frayed and dirty horizon blue uniforms. Harriman pointed to the wooded hills where the scurrying figures had been seen. "Boche?" he asked.
>
> "Oui, Boche," the men in soiled uniforms answered.
>
> "Boche, Paris?" someone asked.
>
> "Oui," the Frenchmen shrugged his shoulders, "ce ne fait rien."[19]

The advancing Germans encountered the 4th Brigade on June 2 and were stopped by the accuracy of the American rifle fire. The doughboys had dug individual holes along the length of their lines, and from these they repulsed the German attack. Though Boyd had a position in these lines, the men of the 75th Company of the 1st Battalion found little reason to fire their rifles that day and complained about not seeing any Germans.[20]

The German army spent the next four days moving artillery pieces to the front and building up defensive positions among the dense trees and rocky ravines of Belleau Wood. The German artillery pieces subjected the men of the 4th Brigade to an almost constant bombardment, and by the time the marines assaulted the wood, the Germans had created a formidable defense with lines of fire covering every approach to the wood.

The Battle of Belleau Wood was the most important battle in which the marines participated during World War I. Despite its limited strategic significance, the battle helped to boost morale and established the marines as a formidable fighting force. The battle provided Boyd with the first opportunity to test his bravery and to prove his valor. During the fighting at Belleau Wood, he and the other marines received their first instruction in offensive modern warfare.

On June 5, 1918, the marine brigade consolidated its position directly in front of Belleau Wood. The brigade's flanks were guarded by re-formed French divisions. The next day, elements of the 5th and 6th Regiments attacked. Battalions from the 5th Marines approached the wood across an open field of wheat and were cut to pieces by murderous enfilading fire, which prevented the 5th from achieving its first-day objectives. The attacking battalions of the 6th were luckier and more successful that first day. Advancing in orderly lines across terrain that provided some protection, they met stiff resistance but made it into the woods. Once under the trees, the fighting became close and fierce. The well-placed German machine guns posed serious problems for the advancing marines and were overcome only by wild headlong attacks. Less than two hours after entering Belleau Wood, the 6th had pushed the Germans out of its southern edge. By the end of the first day of fighting, both the Germans and the Americans had committed and lost too many men to abandon the area.[21]

As a member of the 1st Battalion, Thomas Boyd did not participate in the first day of fighting in Belleau Wood. The attacking group that day was composed of the 2nd and 3rd Battalions while the 1st Battalion was held in reserve. The 3rd Battalion spent the next two days consolidating the marine position inside the wood and inching its lines forward. On June 9, the 1st Battalion, in conjunction with the 2nd Battalion of the 5th Marines, attacked again. The 1st succeeded in driving the Germans from the southern part of Belleau Wood and secured a thin strip of forest that connected it to the larger northern part, which was still in German hands. Casualty rates were high among the marines and the Germans. Between June 11 and 13, the men of the 6th Marines captured four hundred prisoners and sixty machine guns.[22] During this phase of the fighting, Boyd may have come into possession of one of those machine guns and gotten his first close look at a dead German. He described these events in *Through the Wheat:*

> Before him, on a knoll of green, was a pile of heavy boulders, and peeping through a crevice stuck the nose of a Maxim. Climbing the knoll to the right, he looked into the machine gun nest. Three bodies, motionless as the rocks themselves, stretched at length. One had fallen face forward, an arm thrown over the stock of the weapon. His back, that swelled under the gray coat, was turned reproachfully to the sky. Another was sprawled on his back, his hands and legs frozen in a gesture of complete negation. His chin had fallen heavily on his breast and upon his head his small trench cap was tilted forward at a rakish angle. The other man's face was a clot of blood. Death, camera like, had caught and held him fast, his body supported by the rocks, his face like a battered sunflower in the evening.[23]

On June 13, the Germans launched a counterattack that ultimately failed. Throughout the day and night they maintained a steady barrage of high explosive and gas shells against the marine positions within the wood. Boyd's battalion, stationed in the woods and the nearby village of Bourshes, suffered 450 casualties. He was among the few not seriously injured.

Following the counterattack of June 13, the entire 4th Brigade got a short rest behind the lines. During this rest their ranks were reorganized, and

2,800 replacements were brought up. Back at the front a few days later, the marines began the final push that eventually forced the Germans to abandon Belleau Wood and secured the area for the Allies on June 26, 1918. The victorious 4th Brigade received numerous accolades for its part in the victory at Belleau Wood and earned the respect of the German troops, who nicknamed the marines the "Devil Dogs." In addition to praise and admiration, the men of the 4th Brigade received the reward they wanted most, a few weeks' rest away from the fighting.

In mid-July after the men had recuperated, Allied high command moved the 4th Brigade quickly and clandestinely to the Aisne-Marne sector in preparation for one of the most important Allied offensive actions of 1918. On July 18, the 5th Marines and a French regiment attacked the German lines and broke through near the town of Soissons. The 6th Regiment, held in reserve on the eighteenth, led the attack the next day.[24] On July 19, in the face of increasingly heavy resistance, the 6th pushed the Germans almost to the village of Tigny only ten kilometers south of Soissons.[25]

The 6th Marines' part in the Battle of Soissons was a difficult one. They attacked spread out along a 2,500-yard front. Boyd and the 1st Battalion were on the left flank near the French Moroccan Division, and the 2nd Battalion made up the right flank of the attacking wave. Both battalions advanced in plain sight across wheat fields that provided little cover. Their attack was poorly supported by artillery and hindered more than helped by a unit of French tanks. Casualties among the 1st and 2nd Battalions were nearly 50 percent in the first half hour. Reserve companies of the 3rd Battalion had to be rushed forward to bolster their evaporating ranks.[26] Boyd was one of the few in his unit to escape injury. The charge at Soissons is one of the most vividly rendered scenes in *Through the Wheat*:

> The platoon lay down in the wheat, trying to shield their backs from the sight of the enemy. But the tanks, wheeling and rearing and grinding like devils gnashing their teeth, made perfect targets for long range shells. . . . For an everlasting half hour they ploughed and squirmed through the field struggling to get into position so

> that the attack might commence. Meanwhile shells timed like the ticking of a clock fell with horrible and spirit shaking accuracy. At last the tanks had maneuvered themselves into the proper distance ahead of the front line. Whistles were blown piercingly. The advance, men aligned in waves of four, had commenced.
>
> * * *
>
> The whistles blew and Hicks rose again. As he started forward, abreast of the first wave, he had never before felt so great a stiffness in his legs, nor so great a weight in his shoes. It was as if they were tied to the earth. For a moment the jargon and melody of a popular tune flooded his brain.
>
> * * *
>
> "Close in there Hicks," somebody yelled, and Hicks asked whether the men were not being killed fast enough without grouping them together more closely. They advanced to a point where they were enfiladed by the enemies' machine guns. As the four lines had become two, so now the two lines became one. But on they marched, preserving a line that could have passed the reviewing stand on dress parade.
>
> * * *
>
> Under the combination of direct artillery fire, enfilade machine gun, rifle sniping, and bombs dropped from airplanes, the ranks of advancing men had become so sparse that the attack was brought to a temporary halt.[27]

After a long day of fighting, the 6th received orders to dig in where it was and spent part of the night of July 19 in hastily dug foxholes. At midnight a French division moved to the front and relieved the marine brigade, which moved to the rear for a well-deserved rest.[28]

On the last day of the Battle of Soissons, Thomas Boyd performed an act of bravery for which he was awarded the Croix de Guerre. He and fourteen other marines risked their lives by volunteering to carry wounded to safety during a heavy bombardment. The men's bravery was also cited in the 2nd

Division's General Orders.[29] *Through the Wheat* contains no clear description of the action for which Boyd was decorated, but in one scene Hicks helps carry wounded men to a hospital in the rear during a heavy and continuous bombardment. On his last trip from the front to the hospital, Hicks, his partner, and the wounded man are caught in a gas attack. Hicks gives his gas mask to the wounded soldier and spends the rest of the night with his coat over his head calling for help. The next morning when a patrol finds them, the wounded man is dead, and Hicks, unable to speak, passes out.[30]

During a rest period, Boyd witnessed something that would haunt him for years after the war. A young marine who had survived the bitter fighting at Soissons died when a limb from the tree under which he slept fell and crushed his skull. The injustice of this soldier's death remained with Boyd throughout his life, and he included a description of the episode in *Through the Wheat*.[31]

The 6th Regiment's next encounter with the Germans occurred at Saint-Mihiel September 12–16. Attacking in battalion formation, the 2nd Battalion in front with the 1st and 3rd Battalions following, the 6th led the assault on the Saint-Mihiel salient. The regiment distinguished itself in what was a comparatively easy fight and achieved all of its objectives.

In October 1918, the 2nd Division moved to the Meuse-Argonne region near the Hindenburg Line in preparation for an assault on the German stronghold of Mont Blanc.[32] When the marines of the 4th Brigade relieved the tattered remains of a French division at the base of Mont Blanc, they found their position filled with Germans who harassed them until being driven off the following night. As marine commanders surveyed the terrain over which their men would attack, two serious problems presented themselves. On the left, a heavily fortified loop of the German trenches called Essen Hook would allow the Germans to maintain a deadly flanking fire on any advancing units. A small wooded area known as Viper's Wood posed another problem. It stood directly in the middle of the path that the attacking marines would have to take to assault the summit of Mont Blanc, and it contained elements of the German army that would have to be driven out. Unfortunately for the men of the 4th Brigade, there was no easy solution to either problem.

According to the plans for the attack, the 2nd Division would split in two, beginning the assault with a kilometer gap between them, which would allow them to pass on either side of Viper's Wood. The brigade on the left would deal with Essen Hook as best it could. The 6th Marine Regiment was chosen to lead the assault on the left. The attack began on October 3, and despite heavy fire from Essen Hook that inflicted heavy casualties on the attacking marines, the 6th achieved its first-day objectives and drove the Germans from their positions at Mont Blanc. By the time the 6th was relieved on October 10, the 1st Battalion had been reduced to a "handful" of men and all of its officers had been killed or wounded.[33]

Boyd was not among the few remaining members of the 1st Battalion on active duty on October 10. He had been severely gassed on October 6 and sent to a hospital in the rear.[34] *Through the Wheat* contains no description of the event, but Boyd described the experience of being wounded in a gas attack in a short story called "The Long Shot," published in a collection of his war stories, *Points of Honor:*

> A piece of shell casing ripped through the air and Milner's nostrils were bitten by a pungent smell while a saffron kind of liquid splashed towards him. His eyes commenced to smart. He gasped, gulped, and in terror rolled down the gray waste of ground in the direction of his trench.[35]

Boyd spent the rest of his term of enlistment alternately confined to a series of army hospitals in which he underwent treatment for phosgene gas and smoke inhalation and serving guard duty with the army of occupation. He suffered through several illnesses and maladies related to his injuries, including bronchitis, laryngitis, diseased tonsils, and a hysterical spasm of his laryngeal muscles.[36] Boyd rejoined his unit in December 1918.

While in the hospital, Boyd resumed his letter writing. His first letter to his mother since March 1918 obliquely informed her of his injury:

> Dearest Mother,
>
> I suppose that the long interval in between my last letter and this one is causing you some anxiety but you see we have been very actively engaged at the front so I haven't had the opportunity to write. But now I am back in the hospital a blesse' from our last 'push.' But then I have no cause to complain as it took me almost nine long months to get it and besides it isn't very serious. So don't worry.
>
> I have had almost a month in moving from one hospital to another and the beauty of it is, the hospitals improve as I go along. I was brought to this hospital last night and was put to bed. This morning I ate a good breakfast and this noon I had *chicken* for dinner! and tapioca pudding! Can you beat that? It wouldn't have been so surprising if some beatific celestial being in a long flowing white robe had passed it out for then I would have known I was in heaven.[37]

For Boyd, who had spent more time in combat than the vast majority of American soldiers who served in France during the First World War, the time in the hospital offered a welcome relief from the terror, strict discipline, poor food, and squalid living conditions to which he had become accustomed.

As luck would have it, the 2nd Division was chosen to be the army of occupation, and in December 1918 Boyd joined his unit near the city of Cologne. While stationed there he wrote his mother a letter in which he reflected on his luck in having survived the war, looked forward to the day when he would return to the United States, and, for the first time, expressed bitterness about the war:

> I certainly am glad that it is all over because now I am more certain that I'll be home some of these fine days. A few months ago I wouldn't have bet much money one way or the other because they were using our regiment a little too much. . . . I can stand it until I get home. We'll make old Bacchus the god of chow and booze look

> sick when you start making that fried spring chicken à la Maryland and the Thousand Island pudding, the noodles, the—oh lord it makes me feel faint. . . .
>
> But of course our division had to be the army of occupation and so we have the honor of hiking to this beautiful little spot. And now they are experimenting on how long a man can live on nothing to eat. But then we're doing it for democracy and it's a privilege and wave the little flag some more boys we're exempted.[38]

In addition to a new found cynicism, Boyd also for the first time expressed something akin to a political sentiment in regard to press reports that glorified the sobriety and morality of the American soldier:

> I read in the different papers about America's temperance army and America's clean moral army. They make me sick, flaunting the virtues of the poor doughboy in the face of other nations. While we take pride in our cleanliness, as [*sic*] least I don't want to be in a petticoat brigade. In France the beer was no good so we drank wine, cognac, and prunell and when we were relieved after we had had it kind of tough for a few days, why, we naturally would get 'lit up' some. In our platoon there was Walter Lepere, Freddy Davidson, Jerry Daulton, John Fisher, Jen Yeager, and maybe a couple more—and I'll be damned if they're not all dead and not one of them drank a drop.[39]

As Boyd began to take a more realistic view of the world, the United States, and military service, his career in the Marine Corps drew to a close.

Boyd's service in Europe ended on April 4, 1919, when he was shipped home. From the time he arrived in the United States until his honorable discharge on July 10, 1919, he served the Marines Corps from a hospital bed at the U.S. Naval Hospital at Great Lakes, Illinois. He had returned to the United States ahead of his comrades for reasons not made clear by his military record, but possibly related to battle fatigue. On May 31, a doctor at the hospital examined him and Boyd's only complaint was of nervousness. After his discharge he was again examined by a government physician on August 9, 1920, and diagnosed as suffering from hysteria.[40] It seems clear now that Thomas Boyd suffered from some form of post-traumatic stress syndrome. The closing scene of *Through the Wheat* even hints at some sort of psychological breakdown in the novel's main character William Hicks:

> The portly captain walked back and forth behind them, admonishing them to quickness of action. . . .
>
> He paced in front of them offering advice, telling one man to dig a deeper barricade and another not to expose himself. He turned to Hicks, who was lying still, engaged in nothing.
>
> "Are you an automatic rifleman?" he asked. Hicks answered that he was.
>
> "Then take your squad out a couple of hundred yards and establish an outpost. You can't tell when them devils'll come sneakin' up on us."
>
> "Aye, aye, sir." Hicks turned away.
>
> His loader of the night before approached the portly captain.
>
> "Sir, you hadn't better send Hicks out on that outpost."
>
> The captain spat, "Why the devil not?"
>
> "Because, sir, he's crazy. Last night he got to talkin' to dead men, and when they didn't answer he shook them as if he thought they was alive."
>
> "Be off with you," the captain replied, giving the loader no more attention.
>
> Hicks in the lead, the three men started off toward the German lines, to halt half-way, thus to be enabled to inform the platoon if the enemy were attacking. Perhaps four hundreds of yards from the German lines Hicks stopped beside a mound of earth wide enough to conceal the bodies of the three men.
>
> "You fellows lie down here. I've got to get my gun."

> They looked at him agape as he strode toward the enemy's line near which lay his discarded rifle. . . .
>
> Hicks tramped on through the field, dimly sensing the dead, the odors, the scene. He found his rifle where he had thrown it. As he picked it up, the ridge swarmed with small gray figures, ever growing nearer. He turned and walked toward his platoon. The breath from his nostrils felt cool. He raised his chin a little. The action seemed to draw his feet from the earth. No longer did anything matter, neither the bayonets, the bullets, the barbed wire, the dead, nor the living. The soul of Hicks was numb.[41]

At the time of Boyd's discharge, little was known about the effects of combat on the psyches of the combatants, and so the doctors who dealt with Boyd after the war described him as simply nervous or hysterical.

Whether Boyd suffered from post-traumatic stress syndrome or not, his service in the Great War affected him deeply. A photograph taken during his stay with the army of occupation provides a stark contrast to the photo taken before he took ship for France. His uniform is less orderly, his posture is less formal, and his face clearly shows the physical and mental effects of the strain of months of combat. Gone is the confident, open-eyed, eager expression of a bright-faced recruit. In its place is the deeply lined, sunken-eyed face of a man who has had a close look at the horrors of twentieth-century warfare

For Boyd the First World War proved to be the pivotal point of his life. The physical effects of his wounds remained a hindrance to him for the rest of his life, and his wartime experience provided him with the material for much of his best writing. The war forever changed the way he viewed people, the world, and his country.

chapter three

"it was beaten out of the hot metal of . . . experience"

WHILE BOYD RECUPERATED in the Naval Hospital at Great Lakes, Illinois, his mother took a leave from work and came to stay with him. After his discharge, they returned to Defiance together, where Tom enjoyed the food he had looked forward to while in Germany and spent one of the longest uninterrupted periods of his life with his mother. For a while Tom savored being in Ohio again and became reacquainted with his grandfather. But soon, life in Defiance became too constrictive and he decided to strike out on his own to find his place in the world. His restless spirit and desire to find his purpose in life led him across the Midwest and into relationships with people who shaped the rest of his life.

Boyd left Defiance and the company of his family late in the summer of 1919. His paternal grandmother, Elizabeth Boyd, had died and left him a few hundred dollars, and he used this money to move and establish himself in Toledo, Ohio. His Elgin sweetheart, De Ette, had carried out a threat she made to Tom while he was in the marines and married a local drugstore owner. Her rejection affected his ideas of romance and caused him to approach his next few relationships with a good deal of cynicism. In Toledo he met and became involved with a married woman.

His inheritance did not last long. Forced to take a job in a local machine shop to support himself, Boyd gained an appreciation for the plight of the common laborer and a clear understanding of exactly how much harm had been done to his lungs during the war. When he realized that he could not work a twelve-hour shift in a physically demanding job, Tom quit and moved to Chicago, but the injustices he and his coworkers endured at the machine shop influenced his political ideas until the end of his life.[1] In his last novel, a largely autobiographical continuation of the story of William Hicks, the hero of *Through the Wheat*, Boyd expressed these ideas:

> Hicks tightened his lips and stared with resentful determination at the spot beneath the milky stream where the tool bit into the whirling bar. It was no longer a contest between himself and the machine: it was a contest he had to wage against both the machine and the foreman. For the machine was firmly on the foreman's side. As Hicks realized this he also realized that he could never make headway against the combination. It was always the same. Every night, once his sore muscles had limbered up, he worked with increasing strength and confidence till after midnight, when, hour by hour, the machine gained over his tired body. There was only one exhausting, monotonous rhythm which the owners of the machine had imposed—ten hours a day, twelve hours a night.[2]

His social consciousness was just beginning to develop and for the first time he began to question the fairness of the American economic system.

When he got off the train in Chicago, Boyd had no home, no job, little money, and no friends in the city. On his first day in the city he had the good fortune to run into one of his old commanding officers, Colonel Breckinridge, who wrote him a letter of recommendation to the owner of a chain of cigar stores. Boyd went to the address the colonel wrote on the card and was immediately hired as a sales clerk at one of United Cigar Company's area stores. While at the owner's home, he met and charmed the owner's daughter, who was a divorced single mother. Within a few weeks he and the girl were seriously involved, and his future as an executive in the cigar company seemed assured. After a few weeks of settling into his new job and his new relationship, Tom decided to look up his only relative in Chicago, Margaret Woodward "Peggy" Smith.

Peggy Smith was the daughter of Grace and Duncan Smith, the couple who had taken in his parents during his father's illness. Tom and Peggy shared the same great-great-grandfather, William Rohn, which made them third cousins. Her parents had fallen on hard economic times and Peggy had been forced to leave college after only a year. She got a job as a reporter for the *Chicago Daily News*, and several stories had appeared in the paper under her byline. Through the paper, she met and became friends with Ben Hecht and Carl Sandburg. She lived in an apartment with friend and aspiring novelist Rose Caylor. Peggy also wanted to write novels but could not take a long enough break from newspaper reporting to work seriously on the novel she had already started. She decided that the solution to her problem was marriage, but she would have to marry the right sort of man. She ended a serious relationship with a man whose overbearing nature she felt would hinder her efforts to become a novelist. A short time after the breakup she got an invitation to dinner from Tom Boyd.

Their first date coincided with one of the coldest nights of December 1919, but by the time the date was over Thomas Boyd had fallen in love with Peggy and had decided not to marry the cigar store owner's daughter. Peggy was unlike most of the women Tom had known. A petite young woman with dark, curly hair cut short, a flawless complexion, a small straight nose, and blue eyes that danced, Peggy Smith impressed Tom. But what affected him most was her mind and independent spirit. Her status as a working reporter contributed to the sense of awe she inspired in him. During their conversation Tom learned that he and Peggy shared a passion for literature, that she wanted to be an author, and that she was interested in Christian Science. When he confided his desire to be a writer,

Peggy encouraged him and told him she was sure he could find work as a reporter.

For her part, Peggy Smith was less impressed with Tom. She found him very handsome, quiet, and congenial, but she saw little of the intellectual spark that she felt was important in a man. Still, she believed Tom was the kind of man she could control and that would allow her to quit her job as a reporter and pursue a career as a full-time writer. Despite her cynical approach to the relationship, Peggy would quickly grow to love Tom.

Though he knew he would never marry the cigar store owner's daughter, Boyd hesitated to end their relationship. He depended on his income from the cigar store and he feared that breaking the engagement would devastate his fiancée. Alice Boyd and Bob Hepburn encouraged him to stay with his boss's daughter and to forget about Peggy. Alice tried to convince Tom that his fiancée would commit suicide if he broke up with her and told him he would be a fool to give up the career as an executive. She further attempted to influence him by telling him that because he and Peggy were cousins, they would go insane if they had sex and that their children would be horribly deformed. Her campaign to prevent Tom from ending his engagement worked, but she could not keep him from seeing Peggy. For a few months Tom led a double life: seeing Peggy during the day and his fiancée at night.

When it became clear to Alice that Tom's love for Peggy was about to spoil his chances to be an executive, she went to visit Grace Smith and told her about Tom's commitment to the other woman. Grace explained the situation to her daughter, and Peggy, who had grown very fond of Tom, was crushed. She confronted Tom and he confirmed the story. Upset, Peggy left Chicago and went to visit some relatives in Defiance. When she returned, she made it clear to Tom that as long as he remained engaged to the other woman, his relationship with her was at an end. Despite her resolve, her feelings for Tom ran too deep to bear total separation, and she and Tom worked out a way to see each other. They would double date—Peggy with a man other than Tom and Tom with one of Peggy's friends. If any of Peggy's suitors objected to Tom's constant presence, she stopped dating them. This continued until May 1920. On Decoration Day Tom called Peggy and told her that he had broken his engagement with the cigar store owner's daughter.

To fulfill a promise she had made to her mother to spend some time with her family before she married, Peggy moved to Minneapolis in June 1920 to live with Grace and Duncan Smith. Duncan Smith's Nebraska newspaper had failed and he had been forced to take a job as a columnist for a Twin Cities paper. Her appearance on her parents' doorstep was something of a shock to her parents, but she kept her reasons for relocating a secret. While Boyd remained in Chicago to help her roommate find a new apartment and move, Peggy looked for a place near her parents' house for him and attempted to prepare her parents for his arrival.[3] Just before Tom moved to Minneapolis, Peggy wrote him to apprise him of the situation:

> My dad doesn't think you can get on a paper here. He says that the Minnesota newspapers aren't educational institutions. Tommy, I know you can get on. He always talks that way, and he told me that I was absolutely nutty to ever try to get on a paper when I first started out. So he always discourages everybody. I'm afraid he won't help you much. But I'll help you, and I know you will get on.
>
> My father of course wanted to know why you were coming up. To which I replied, "How should I know?" He then asked in a sort of disgusted way whether or not you had any more idea than Ward had about the economic forces that were moving the world. Do read up Tommy, on economic determinism, industrial unionism, Marxian socialism, the Fabian Society, and the life of Eugene V. Debs.
>
> I asked him whether he didn't want you to come or not, and he said gloomily that he didn't care. . . . I said you weren't as bad as Ward, that you were quite nice. He cheered up at that and said that your father was a nice chap and he would like to see you. Your father was really a fine man, he said, and seemed quite a lot brightened in spirits.

> Tommy, when you do come up, you mustn't lose a minute in starting out seriously to work, will you? (This a little of the advice I promised you.) I have a room for you, two doors away for five dollars a week. . . . You can change it if you don't like it. I thought it would do for the present as it is near us and everything.[4]

A few days after receiving the letter, Tom moved into the room near the Smiths and shortly after his arrival, he and Peggy announced their engagement.

As Peggy advised, Tom began to look for work almost immediately. Perhaps more influenced by Duncan Smith's belief in his chances of getting a job as a reporter than Peggy's and with serious doubts about his ability to write, Tom refused to apply at any of the local newspapers and instead looked for work as a store clerk. He found a job selling men's apparel in a discount clothing shop. His pay barely covered his weekly expenses, and he was unable to save any money or find a better position.[5] One night, while visiting the Smith household, Tom expressed his frustration with his situation by jokingly telling Peggy that he was thinking of becoming a Bolshevik. She immediately led him to her father's study, where Duncan Smith introduced him to the works of Karl Marx and the tenets of socialism. From that point until the 1930s, Thomas Boyd considered himself a theoretical socialist.[6] He and Peggy often discussed socialist philosophy, and they judged people they met based on their social awareness. After they were married, Tom scandalized some of his wealthier friends by going to hear Socialist Party leader William Z. Foster give a speech.

Whatever her socialist beliefs, Peggy understood that if she and Tom were ever going to get married, and if she was ever going to be able to complete her novel, Tom would have to get a job that paid a good deal more that he was making at the resale shop. She felt confident that he could get a job as a reporter on a new paper, the *Non-Partisan Leaguer,* and made up her mind that Tom would apply. Boyd remained reluctant, convinced that he could not write and would never get the job. Faced with Tom's adamant refusal to apply, Peggy worked out a plan to trick him into doing so. She asked him to meet her for lunch in downtown Minneapolis and gave him directions to the restaurant. Instead of finding Peggy waiting for him in front of a restaurant, he found her outside the offices of the new newspaper. She had to drag him into the building and into the offices of the editor. She introduced herself as a reporter for the *Chicago Daily News*, told the editor that Tom was one of the finest reporters that paper had ever had, and advised him to hire Tom on the spot. Whether the editor was fooled by Peggy's ruse or just needed to find people capable of filing reports, he hired Tom and agreed to pay him twenty-five dollars a week.

They were both elated. Tom's salary at the paper would be far more than he had been making and more than enough to allow Peggy to begin making definite wedding plans. In addition, Tom would finally be doing something that he really wanted to do. But the thrill of getting the job faded, and Tom sank into a depression. Believing that he would never be able to write well enough to fool the editors, Tom convinced himself that he would be fired the first day. Peggy, to whom writing had always come easily, thought he was being silly. To prove that he could write she made up a situation and had Tom try to put together a story. When he failed Peggy's test, Tom's depression worsened.

Fortunately, when Boyd reported for work at the offices of the *Non-Partisan Leaguer*, the editor assigned him to work with an experienced reporter named James Fitzgerald at St. Paul's central police station. Instead of writing the stories himself, Boyd called in the facts of interesting cases to the newspaper, where another reporter would actually write the story. For six weeks he sat around a card table at the police station playing cards, occasionally getting up to gather facts about a police matter or to follow the police to a crime scene and then phone in the details to the newspaper offices. After a few weeks, his confidence had grown and he attempted to write a story of his own. When his work was praised, he began to write more. He wrote passionately about cases involving injustices, a sign of his burgeoning social consciousness. Boyd soon learned that the key was to write about subjects on which he had strong feelings. For the rest of his writing life, his best work would always be on subjects that were close to his heart.

As stories began to appear in the *Non-Partisan Leaguer* under Tom's byline, Peggy decided that Tom should move to a more prestigious newspaper. At her insistence, Boyd met with the editors of the *St. Paul Daily News*, who offered to hire him at five dollars a week more than he had been making. He went to work for the *Daily News* in mid-October 1921.

The extra five dollars a week convinced Tom and Peggy that they could finally afford to get married. The ceremony took place at City Hall in Minneapolis on October 20, 1921. Peggy wore a dark green silk dress embroidered with gold and Tom wore his best blue suit. Afterward they were taken to lunch by Peggy's parents. They dined at one of Minneapolis's most expensive hotels, but no one particularly enjoyed the meal.[7] Boyd later recreated the scene in *In Time of Peace*:

> In the mouldering splendor of thick columns, red plush carpet, and floridly painted ceiling they sat down to the wedding feast—two eager youngsters still unaware of what had happened to them, two older people, grave and hopeful, but none of them very wise.
>
> Throughout supper Mrs. Hughes preserved her manner of strict judicious calm. Mr. Hughes, ruddy faced, fumbled with knife and fork, with napkin, coffee spoon, and rank cigar. . . . Mr. Hughes looked anxiously at his wife, mutely demanding some word of guidance for Patsy, some helpful advice from their joint experience. But Mrs. Hughes gazed back helpless and inarticulate.[8]

Despite the formal and tense relationship implied by this scene, Tom and Peggy remained on good terms with the Smiths and visited them often. Tom and Peggy, at least in correspondence to one another, referred to one another's parents in terms of their non-married relationship to them: Peggy called Tom's mother Aunt Alice and Tom called Peggy's parents Aunt Grace and Uncle Duncan.

The newlyweds settled into a third-floor apartment at 391 Selby Avenue in St. Paul. The flat was small. All of the rooms opened directly off the main sitting room through one of a number of doors which gave the room a strange appearance and little wall space. One door opened onto a small balcony, and from the window in the sitting room, the roofs of the surrounding buildings and the spire of St. Paul's Catholic Cathedral could be seen. They were happy. Boyd enjoyed his new job with the *Daily News* and Peggy began serious work on her novel. After only a few months of marriage, Peggy became pregnant, and she and Tom realized that raising a baby in the apartment would be a practical impossibility. They found a cheap bungalow for sale on the outskirts of St. Paul. With the help of Duncan Smith they were able to finance a mortgage and moved into the bungalow at 2115 Randolph Street. The house, which was brown and sat on a thick raised slab, consisted of one big L-shaped room which could be divided, by hanging curtains, into a separate sitting room, dining room, kitchen, and bedroom. There was a cornfield across the street from the house and the river was nearby. Boyd would spend many hours trying to grow a garden in the yard and enjoyed the relatively rural setting. Despite the fact that he had to walk more than a mile to where the trolley car tracks ended and then ride into work, he loved their new home.

Work on the novel and pregnancy did not consume all of Peggy's time while the Boyds lived on Randolph Street. She continued to think of ways to improve Tom's position and income. A man she had known while she worked for the *Chicago Daily News* had started a page in that paper devoted strictly to news, reviews, and the discussion of books. His page was supported completely by advertisements from publishers and local bookstores, and he had become quite successful. Peggy decided that Tom should propose to his editors the creation of a similar page that he would write and edit. Typically reluctant, Tom only agreed to the idea after Peggy assured him that she would help him to complete the weekly literary supplement. Though initially reluctant, Tom's employers agreed to give his book page a trial run.

In a Corner with the Bookworm premiered on page 6 of the City Life section of the *St. Paul Daily News* in November 1920. It would remain a feature of the Sunday paper until 1923. Though Tom's name appeared alone at the top of the page, Peggy wrote or transcribed Tom's thoughts to create most of the material that appeared on the book page for the first three months. As the months passed Boyd contributed more material, but he would not complete a page on his own until November 1921 when Peggy was unable to help him because she was in the hospital giving birth. As his words and ideas came to dominate the page, it became more substantial and serious.

Being the de facto literary editor of the *St. Paul Daily News* came with certain perks of which Boyd took full advantage. One benefit of the new position was an almost immediate introduction into the small but active St. Paul literary community. He and Peggy were invited to join a loose affiliation of Twin Cities writers and journalists who called themselves the Nimbus Club. Club meetings were informal and usually consisted of dinner at a local Italian restaurant, drinking, and retiring to the office of one of the members where they talked, argued, listened to someone play the piano, and sang. The Nimbus Club included local authors Larry Ho (Laurence Hodgson, who was at one point the mayor of St. Paul), Donald Ogden Stewart (later a famous screenwriter), Robert Cary, and the dean of St. Paul writers, Charles Macomb Flandrau. Flandrau wrote literary and dramatic criticism for the *St. Paul Pioneer Press* and had written a collection of humorous travel essays. He and Boyd became good friends, and Flandrau influenced Boyd's literary tastes and introduced him to works of nineteenth-century literature. Later, Boyd collected some of Flandrau's writing and attempted to get it published. Though Boyd failed to find a publisher, the collection, called *Loquacities*, was eventually published.

Cornelius Van Ness, a young, wealthy St. Paul businessman who had an interest in literature, occasionally attended the Nimbus Club meetings; he and Boyd became good friends. Van Ness wanted to open a small bookstore in St. Paul but did not want to have to run it. He wanted to travel Europe searching for rare books and unpublished manuscripts. Boyd, who was aware of a government program that paid veterans fifty dollars a week to learn a trade, offered to manage the store at no expense to Van Ness. Kilmarnock Book Store opened for business at 84 East 4th Street in 1921. This first location was on the second floor of an office building near the editorial offices of the *St. Paul Daily News*. They moved the store to the corner of 4th and Cedar Streets a short time later. The bookstore soon became a hangout for local and visiting authors. Boyd established an eclectic atmosphere in the store: books were arranged according to the color of their bindings rather than by author, there was a fireplace and leather chairs, and his friends and visitors met for tea in the afternoon. He occasionally insulted the local society ladies who came into the store and asked for the latest bestseller and expressed frustration at the lack of literary sophistication of the store's clientele. He was not a good manager.[9]

In 1922, Boyd and Van Ness flirted with the idea of becoming publishers. That year they published *Historica Calaminatum*, a collection of Peter Abelard's letters translated by Henry Adams Bellows with an introduction by Ralph Adams Cram. The expense involved in the publication of this book convinced them not to publish any other books.[10]

Although In a Corner with the Bookworm changed considerably in its three years of existence, it consisted primarily of a literary gossip column called The Literary Punch Bowl, news of the local libraries, correspondence from notable authors, book reviews by the local literati and eventually Boyd himself, and interviews and profiles of the authors he met in St. Paul or while visiting New York and Chicago.

Entries in The Literary Punch Bowl covered a wide range of topics, but were usually culled from other literary reviews or transcribed from conversations Tom or Peggy had with their friends. Often the column was filled with silly statements or scenarios related to the world of publishing:

> We haven't read the "Mirrors of Downing Street" by a 'gentleman with a duster,' but in as much as there seems to be some doubt as to the identity of the author we suggest Lloyd George's butler might have written it.[11]

Occasionally, Tom and Peggy used the column to express their disdain for the literary tastes of the local citizenry:

> The culture snatchers are taking advantage of the friendly weather to trek home afoot with a book in their hands. As we usually walk,

> our powers of observation are becoming stronger everyday. Yesterday for instance we were able to see that copies of "Main Street" are slowly trickling into St. Paul.[12]

But for the most part, The Literary Punchbowl contented itself with literary name-dropping:

> A friend returned from New York, where she teaed with Miss Willa Cather, reports a fondness on the part of Miss Cather for Theodore Dreiser and Sherwood Anderson. A literary fondness it might be added.[13]

Tom and Peggy decided early on that the way to make the book page a success was to fill it with the names of as many well-known authors as possible.

Before Tom even proposed the idea for the book page to his editors, Peggy had the brilliant idea of filling it with correspondence from famous authors. Boyd would write to the authors requesting copy on a particular topic and then publish whatever they wrote back. To his surprise, many of the authors he contacted were more than happy to write him back. Over the years, In a Corner with the Bookworm contained letters written to Boyd from Charles Norris, Zona Gale, Willa Cather, Theodore Dreiser, Carl Sandburg, Sherwood Anderson, H. L. Mencken, Sinclair Lewis, and F. Scott Fitzgerald. Fitzgerald was among the first to respond:

> This writing of a young man's novel consists chiefly in dumping all your youthful adventures into the readers' lap with a practiced air of importance, keeping carefully within the formulas of Wells and Joyce. It seems to me that when accomplished by a man without distinction of style it reaches the depths of banality.[14]

Many authors who wrote to Boyd did so to thank him for a review, plug their next book, or make a statement of their literary philosophy. In 1921 Charles Norris wrote:

> Many thanks for your sympathetic review of "Brass." It is a great comfort to an author when a critic shows he understands what the author is trying to say. . . . I truly believe that the book with a purpose lies outside the province of the novelist. If I can hold the "mirror up to nature" and to do so honestly and sincerely, I shall feel I have accomplished all I set out to do.[15]

Other authors, whom Boyd had met while they were in St. Paul, wrote chatty letters detailing their plans for future books. These letters had little literary value and were not always intended for publication. In October 1922 Sinclair Lewis wrote:

> Your review of "Babbitt" was damn interesting—more than just an outline as most reviews are.
>
> Glad to know I'll be in St. Paul in January—Teakins had not told me. Plan for a party including Grace and Blair Flandrau.
>
> We've taken this house for a year—quite between my bats—last evening I sat before a big log fire reading Huxley's "Crome Yellow."
>
> Mostly loafing.
>
> "Babbitt" starts well. Gran' letters from H. G. Wells, May Sinclair, and Edith Wharton. Did you see what Mencken said about it in the October Smart Set?
>
> Coming East?[16]

While many of the authors' letters were self-aggrandizing, Boyd made sure to include all the letters that made favorable mention of the book page or his skill as a reviewer. Boyd was good at the job of literary editor and able to make connections with celebrity writers.

Like most literary pages, In a Corner with the Bookworm contained weekly reviews of new books. In the early days of the page, most of the reviews were written by Peggy under the pen name of Woodward Boyd or by Boyd's St. Paul literary acquaintances. Local writers Bernard Vaughn,

Robert Cary, and Donald Ogden Stewart contributed reviews as well as St. Paul mayor Lawrence Hodgson (Larry Ho). As Boyd assumed greater control, his opinions and reviews became dominant. He usually wrote reviews only of books he liked. Among his better appraisals were his reviews of *Babbitt* and *Ulysses*. Of *Babbitt* Boyd wrote:

> In "Main Street" Sinclair Lewis was able to interpret the small middle-western scene because he inherently belonged to the scene. He has been successful in "Babbitt" partly for the same reason: there is a great deal of George F. Babbitt in Sinclair Lewis, a George F. Babbitt who apprehends his own faults and is capable of dealing with them caustically. As one finishes this new novel there is a feeling, slightly nebulous, that Mr. Lewis has written much that is autobiography, autobiography of his other self, his unconscious as the psychoanalyst would call it.
>
> And the implication is not that Mr. Lewis has the undesirable qualities so much as the desirable ones.[17]

The review of *Babbitt* was typical of the style and tone of Boyd's criticism. He often heaped praise on the novelists with whom he had become friends. In October 1922, a review of the original Shakespeare and Company edition of James Joyce's *Ulysses* that was anything but typical appeared on the book page. After a careful and thorough dissection of the book and its characters, Boyd passed final judgment on *Ulysses* and James Joyce:

> I believe that Mr. Joyce has surpassed the imaginative efforts of Dr. Francois Rabelais, that he has developed a method of characterization and of working in background through the thoughts of the characters which is the greatest contribution to the expansion of the novel that these later centuries had seen, that "Ulysses" is one of the wittiest works ever written, that it is not at all immoral, that its influence upon the modern novel will be tremendous and also bad because his followers will follow his weaknesses rather than his

> strengths, that it is the most astonishing work I have read since the King James version of the Holy Bible.[18]

Boyd's review of *Ulysses* marked the completion of his transformation from a timid young man with no self-esteem to a confident man sure of his opinions and unafraid to state them.

One factor that contributed to Boyd's growing self-assurance was the association with famous authors provided by his tenure as literary editor of the *St. Paul Daily News*. Whenever authors of note came to St. Paul, Boyd arranged to meet them. In his capacity as literary editor he met and interviewed Carl Sandburg, Sinclair Lewis, Willa Cather, and Sherwood Anderson. The authors, who knew nothing of Boyd's insecurities, treated him with respect. Invariably, Boyd's personal charm and unabashed respect for these authors won them over, and several played an important role in Boyd's future.

Boyd wrote several pieces for the book page detailing these interviews, the most ambitious of which were two three-part profiles called "Literary Libels." One of these "Literary Libels" covered Boyd's meeting with Carl Sandburg. During their breakfast meeting, he and Sandburg discussed the Mississippi River, the poetry of Li Po and Robert Frost, and the poor quality of American coffee. Boyd wove a great deal of background information about Sandburg into the piece to give his readers an overall impression of Sandburg rather than just a transcript of their conversation.[19] In another installment of "Literary Libels" Boyd detailed his meeting with the man who would become, for a time, his sponsor and most important supporter.

Boyd met and gathered well-wishers and friends from the cream of American authors of his day. He could count on advice and support from Sandburg, Anderson, and Lewis. But of all the literary friends Thomas Boyd made, none would be as important to him as F. Scott Fitzgerald.

Scott and Zelda Fitzgerald moved from Montgomery, Alabama, to the cooler climes of St. Paul in the summer of 1921. They rented a house in the suburbs on White Bear Lake and quickly moved into St. Paul society. Scott intended to spend his days revising the manuscript of *The Beautiful and the Damned*, and Zelda was pregnant with their first child.[20] As soon as he learned the general location of the Fitzgeralds' home, Boyd and Cornelius Van Ness took a cab to the suburbs in search of Fitzgerald. He eventually found the house and interviewed Fitzgerald.[21] That same week, he wrote a complete description of the meeting for the book page.

According to "Literary Libels: Francis Scott Key Fitzgerald," Fitzgerald's healthy and robust appearance surprised Boyd, who expected him to be pale, sickly, and dissipated by alcohol. For his part Fitzgerald expressed surprise at Boyd's youth and indicated that he expected Tom to be much older. During their interview the conversation ranged from Fitzgerald's work on the revision of his new novel, to the poor quality of the serialization of that novel which had already appeared in the *Metropolitan* magazine, to the importance of H. L. Mencken, and the poetry of Carl Sandburg. When Boyd asked Fitzgerald why he had decided to become a writer, Fitzgerald claimed that he had been inspired by a novel by Hugh Walpole: "After reading about 100 pages I thought, 'if this fellow can get away with it as an author I can too.'"[22] During their initial meeting Boyd and Fitzgerald connected on some basic level. Van Ness later described the atmosphere in the room when the two men met as almost electric.[23]

The immediate connection between Tom and Scott grew into a deeper friendship after the Fitzgeralds moved to an apartment near Summit Avenue in St. Paul.[24] Fitzgerald became a frequent visitor to Kilmarnock Books. Once, he burst into the store and excitedly proclaimed that he had just walked several blocks down the street with his eyes shut pretending to be blind and had made it all the way without incident. Other circumstances also helped bring the two men into contact with one another. Peggy Boyd and Zelda Fitzgerald were patients at the same St. Paul hospital during the birth of their first children. Scottie Fitzgerald and Betty Grace Boyd were born during the same week of November 1921. To celebrate the births of their children, Fitzgerald threw a party in honor of the mothers; but according to Boyd family legend, Zelda's envy of Peggy's quickly returning figure spoiled the festivities.[25]

Whatever tensions may have existed between their wives, Tom and Scott remained good friends. Boyd became one of Fitzgerald's most ardent supporters and defenders. He used the book page to promote Fitzgerald's work and dispel rumors of his wild behavior. In February 1922, Scott wrote his editor, Maxwell Perkins, noting that his name had appeared on Boyd's book page more than forty times and that Tom had made extraordinary efforts, including the production of a short film to be shown in movie theaters, to advertise the release of *The Beautiful and the Damned*.[26] Fitzgerald repaid Boyd's kindnesses, in part, by writing reviews for the book page. In all he wrote three reviews—of John Dos Passos's *Three Soldiers*, Booth Tarkington's *Gentle Julia*, and Aldous Huxley's *Crome Yellow*—which appeared in the spring of 1922. He also played a major role in the fulfillment of Tom and Peggy's dreams of becoming published authors.

Throughout her pregnancy Peggy Boyd had continued to work on her novel. She called her book *The Love Legend*. It followed the lives of four sisters—Anita, Ward, Sari, and Dizzy—and their experiences with love. In the novel Peggy attempted to dispel the myth that a woman's happiness and security rested on her ability to find the right man and that marriage would fulfill all of a woman's dreams. Shortly after giving birth, she put the finishing touches on her manuscript and began to think about sending it out to publishers. Tom, who thought the book was wonderful, encouraged Peggy to show it to Fitzgerald, but Peggy was convinced that Zelda would poison his opinion. Reluctantly, she agreed to let Boyd show it to Fitzgerald.[27] To her surprise, Fitzgerald loved it and wrote an extensive letter of praise and advice:

> I liked the book immensely. The affair of Ward and Oz is excellent—so is almost all of books III and IV. I have no doubt that Scribner will take it if you change these long lectures and monologues. I will write them a letter. I enjoyed reading the book immensely and think it a remarkable 1st novel.[28]

He followed these words of praise with several pages of specific advice, referenced by page numbers, on ways to improve the novel.

Peggy followed Fitzgerald's suggestions in revising the manuscript, and in January 1922 sent it to Charles Scribner's and Sons. On March 10, 1922,

Max Perkins wrote to inform her of Scribner's decision to publish *The Love Legend*. According to the contract, Peggy would earn a 10 percent royalty on the first 5,000 copies sold and a 15 percent royalty on all copies sold above 5,000.

Perkins planned to bring the book out in fall of 1922, but Peggy's working situation and health delayed publication.[29] Peggy had gone to work for the *Minneapolis Star*. The syndicate to which the *Star* belonged sent her to Columbia, Missouri, and to St. Louis in the spring of 1922.[30] Making matters worse, in June she took Betty Grace to Aurora, Illinois, to visit her parents.[31] By then the proofs of *The Love Legend* had already been sent to St. Paul.[32] In addition to the difficulties posed by her frequent travels, Peggy was pregnant again and was experiencing complications. From Aurora, Peggy wrote Tom to report that she had seen a doctor after a "scare" related to the pregnancy and that the doctor had informed her that the complications of this pregnancy were the result of treatment she had been given after giving birth to Betty Grace.[33] Despite the doctor's assurances that she would be fine, Peggy continued to experience difficulties with her second pregnancy.

Scribner's was not able to complete production of *The Love Legend* until the end of October 1922.[34] The critical community received it enthusiastically. Fitzgerald, naturally, wrote a very positive review for the *New York Post*, comparing the novel to *Babbitt*.[35] The reviewer for the *New York Times* wrote, "'The Love Legend' is a clearly written tale and one which shows much promise."[36] The critic for the *Chicago Daily News* said, "We would say that for a first novel this book is something of an achievement. Fitzgerald is the only author one can draw on for comparison."[37] Peggy received a personal letter of praise and advice from Sinclair Lewis: "I do think it is a very remarkable first novel—or no, let us say just novel, without dragging in the first. I do think that it proves beyond question your vocation for the long, often boring, always wearing vocation of the novelist." Though the rest of his letter was somewhat critical of certain parts of *The Love Legend*, the overall tone was laudatory.[38] If the critics appreciated *The Love Legend* and Peggy Boyd's potential as a writer, the book-buying public paid little attention.

The midwestern papers made much of her beauty and youth, and in St. Paul and Chicago the book sold well, but nationwide it was less successful.

While Peggy traveled from Chicago to St. Louis on newspaper business during the spring and summer of 1922, Tom remained in St. Paul. They wrote one another frequently and complained whenever there was an extended period during which they received no letters. They interspersed their news of work, friends, and family with adolescent proclamations of love and symbolic kisses. When Peggy became ill and the pregnancy was threatened, Tom expressed true fear and concern. In June 1922, while Peggy was living in Aurora, he got a chance to do some traveling of his own. He made a trip to New York on business for the bookshop and to interview authors for the book page and help expedite the publication of *The Love Legend*.[39]

In New York, Boyd met with many authors and publishing executives. His most important meetings were with Sinclair Lewis and Max Perkins. On June 16, he and Perkins met for lunch at the Harvard Club and discussed *The Love Legend* and Peggy's plans for another novel. When Boyd mentioned that he was thinking of writing his own book about his experiences in the Great War, Perkins showed an interest and encouraged Tom to send the manuscript to him when it was completed. Boyd had lunch with Lewis the next day and Lewis also encouraged him to write a book about his experiences. With the encouragement of two men whose opinions he respected, Boyd made up his mind to do what he had wanted to do since he was a teenager. He returned to St. Paul in July determined to write a novel of his own.[40]

When he got back to the bungalow on Randolph Street, Peggy and Betty Grace were already home. Taking little notice of them or anything else, Boyd began writing almost immediately. Well into her second pregnancy, caring for a teething baby, and suffering through a scorching summer, Peggy was incapable of helping Tom or even reading what he had written. Though he wrote wherever he happened to be, Boyd did most of the work on his novel in the back room of Kilmarnock Books. He often neglected his duties as store manager and he spent one night writing by the light from the hallway outside his office. He completed the manuscript of *Through the Wheat* in six weeks.[41] Of the writing of the book, Boyd's friend and partner Cornelius Van Ness wrote, "[I]t was beaten out of the hot metal of an intensely consuming and vividly close by experience; it was carefully and painstakingly put together, but quickly so that nothing had a chance to get cold, and above all it had the thing coursing through it which was youth and which was Tom."[42]

Of all Boyd's books, *Through the Wheat* is perhaps the most self-consciously artful. With his descriptions of the natural surroundings, the quality of light, and even the activities of ants on a battlefield, Boyd was clearly attempting to strike the same naturalistic notes that Stephen Crane struck in *The Red Badge of Courage*. But despite the occasionally heavy handed attempts at literary fireworks, the simple story at the heart of *Through the Wheat* is what comes through. The plot follows Boyd's fictional alter ego William Hicks from early guard duty in France through a sort of emotional breakdown following the Battle of Soissons. While the characters often express disgust with food, officers, and YMCA men, there are few passages in which any of the characters address the morality of war. Because *Through the Wheat* is primarily an autobiographical novel, it is narrowly focused, free of moralizing and obvious messages, and an accurate description of the actions of the 75th Company of the 6th Marine Regiment.

After a quick revision, the manuscript was ready to be sent to a publisher. Boyd decided to send it to Harcourt Brace first. Sinclair Lewis had not only encouraged Boyd to write but had mentioned his book to editor Harrison Smith at Harcourt Brace. In fact, at Lewis's behest Smith had written Boyd a letter and invited him to submit anything he wrote.[43] Lewis's action on Boyd's behalf was based totally on friendship: he had not read the manuscript, and he took no other steps to insure the publication of *Through the Wheat*.[44] In September, Smith wrote Boyd to inform him that Harcourt Brace would not be publishing his book:

> We have read "Through the Wheat" with a great deal of interest; and while it is well to come out bluntly with the statement that we

> are not going to publish it, it will be of aid to you to know that it showed, to our minds, so much merit that we will be extremely interested in anything else you may do. . . . To be perfectly frank, we cannot at present time see a large enough audience for this book.[45]

Disappointed, but not deterred by this initial rejection, Boyd sent the manuscript to Perkins at Scribner's. On October 4, Boyd received Perkins's response. Scribner's would not publish *Through the Wheat.* In the letter of rejection, Perkins, like Smith, cited the perceived lack of a market for the book as the reason for Scribner's rejection. He praised the book, expressed true regret that it could not be accepted, and invited Boyd to submit other work.[46] Crushed by this second rejection and feeling that if his contacts at Harcourt Brace and Scribner's could not help him get into print, *Through the Wheat* would never be published, Boyd fired off an angry letter to Perkins in which he expressed his disappointment:

> It is very definitely a war book the like of which had not been written . . . by . . . anyone else whose work I have come across. . . . I think that the belief that people are sick of war books is false. They are tired of books which use war as a background. The same thing was said when *Three Soldiers* was published. But it went, and well. Because it was a different kind of war book. And so is this again.[47]

Thomas Boyd had overcome his self-doubt and written a novel he passionately believed deserved publication only to have it rejected by the two publishing houses in which he had put the most hope. He now believed that if *Through the Wheat* remained unpublished, he would never be able to write anything worthy of publication.

Boyd's personal life around the time of these rejections offered him no relief. Like many men after the birth of their first child, Tom felt trapped. Suddenly, he was a father with a responsibility to support a wife and a child. These feelings of responsibility manifested themselves in a cold indifference toward his daughter Betty Grace. Peggy felt that his attitude resulted from his disappointment at not having a son, and she worried about his lack of affection for his daughter. Tom remained distant from Betty Grace until a newspaper friend visited the bungalow on Randolph Street with his toddler. When the boy picked up an iron poker and began to run around the house with it held over his head, endangering Betty Grace, who was crawling on the floor, Boyd snatched up his child and angrily confronted his friend. Apparently this incident snapped him out of his depression-induced period of parental neglect, because from that point on he was an attentive and loving parent. Unfortunately, a certain underlying selfishness of his nature, perhaps born in the difficult circumstances of his youth, prevented Boyd from devoting the same amount of care to his marriage.[48]

After months of pregnancy punctuated by illness, fears of miscarriage, and physical pain, Peggy's second pregnancy ended in the stillbirth of twin boys. She fell ill immediately and sank into a deep depression. Tom, who was as usual more than a little self-absorbed, provided Peggy with little comfort; an emotional distance grew between them. As both became increasingly unhappy, tensions rose in their home. Peggy decided that the only way to prevent another child-birthing tragedy was to abstain from sex. This heightened Boyd's sense of unhappiness, and he soon sought comfort in the arms of another woman.

Her name was Sandra and she was the wife of a wealthy St. Paul businessman. An occasional guest at Nimbus Club meetings, Sandra fell for Tom's blond-haired, blue-eyed intensity. She gave Tom a feeling of acceptance and peace that he was missing at home.[49] Years later he described these feelings through his fictional alter ego William Hicks in his last novel, *In Time of Peace:*

> When she had made love full and irresponsible for him again, so generous it had already banished all those pinched and cautious days? How could he be sorry? He was not depriving Patsy [Peggy] of anything. . . .
>
> Hicks felt that as Carlotta's lover he would be released from the goading anxieties of which his life was made.[50]

Though neither Tom nor Peggy ever mentioned Sandra's last name, a local woman named Alexandra (Xandra) Kallman could have been Tom's lover. She was the wife of the well-to-do St. Paul banker Oscar Kallman and associated with literary people. The Kallmans, like the Boyds, befriended the Fitzgeralds when they moved to St. Paul in 1921. The Kallmans had been the ones who helped Scott and Zelda secure a residence in the city when they moved from the home they were renting on White Bear Lake, and Xandra paid frequent visits to Zelda while she was in the hospital before and after the birth of Scottie Fitzgerald. After the Fitzgeralds left Minnesota in 1922, Xandra and Zelda continued to correspond. In her letters, Zelda often spelled Xandra's name with an *S* instead of an *X*, Sandra instead of Xandra.[51] Whoever Sandra was, she was only the first of several women with whom Tom had affairs during his marriage to Peggy. Boyd seems to have had a flaw in his character that led him to seek out other women when things at home became difficult or when the responsibilities of marriage became overwhelming.

In October 1922, the Boyds moved closer to the center of St. Paul, taking up residence in a flat at 604 Summit Avenue. Though he now lived closer to the newspaper's offices and the bookstore, the literary scene in St. Paul had lost some of its charm. The Fitzgeralds had moved to Great Neck, New York, Sinclair Lewis's visits to St. Paul had stopped, and Charles Flandrau was on an extended trip to Europe.[52] Boyd continued to write the book page and manage Kilmarnock Books, but he had little hope of establishing himself as a working author.

In early November, he received a postcard from Fitzgerald consoling him about *Through the Wheat* and asking Boyd to send the manuscript to Great Neck so he could read it.[53] He mailed the manuscript, but did not believe that Fitzgerald would be able to help. Then on December 13, 1922, he received a telegram from Max Perkins and F. Scott Fitzgerald: "Our enthusiasm for your book was such that Mr. Scribner caught it. It is to be published."[54] A letter from Fitzgerald written that same day explained how the reversal of *Through the Wheat*'s fortunes had come about.

After receiving the manuscript, Fitzgerald left it at a friend's house where it remained unread for two weeks while the friend was on vacation. When he had retrieved the book and read it, Fitzgerald immediately became the book's biggest fan. Convinced that it deserved publication, he decided to try to get it serialized in a magazine. But before taking it to any magazine editors, he called Perkins at his Scribner's office to tell him how wonderful he thought Boyd's book was. He quickly learned that Perkins had been for publication of *Through the Wheat* all along. In a bold move, Perkins asked Fitzgerald to come immediately to the Scribner's offices for a meeting with Charles Scribner Sr. At that meeting Fitzgerald's enthusiasm for *Through the Wheat* won over Mr. Scribner, and he decided in favor of publication.[55]

That Fitzgerald, the darling of young American readers and the fair-haired boy of American authors, should take such extraordinary steps on behalf of a young, unknown newspaper editor from the Midwest was not as unusual as it sounds; in fact, it was completely in keeping with Fitzgerald's character. Fitzgerald enjoyed playing talent scout for Scribner's. Over the course of his career, he introduced several writers to Scribner's, including the Boyds, Ring Lardner, and Ernest Hemingway.[56] Boyd's efforts to promote Fitzgerald's work, his defense of Fitzgerald's character on the book page, and his eagerness to learn from Fitzgerald endeared him to Scott and helped forge a strong bond between them.[57] In addition, Fitzgerald undoubtedly admired Boyd's war record. Throughout his life, Fitzgerald expressed disappointment over his failure to have the opportunity to lead men in battle and exhibit heroism.[58] All of these factors explain Fitzgerald's friendship with Boyd and his offer to read *Through the Wheat*, but it was the quality of the manuscript that ultimately convinced him to plead its case before Charles Scribner Sr.

Boyd recognized and acknowledged the role Fitzgerald played in the acceptance of *Through the Wheat* in a letter of thanks he wrote Scott shortly after receiving word of the novel's acceptance:

> To attempt to tell you of my honest gratitude would only show up my inability to express myself. When Scribner's turned down "Through the Wheat" I cried in reading the letter of rejection—as I also did when I wrote certain parts of the book. And besides, I felt that so long as it remained unpublished I could never write anything else;

> the best of which I am capable is in "Through the Wheat" and to dam [*sic*] that would be to dam all subsequent transcriptions of thought and experiences. I feel quite aware that it is only through you and your inexhaustible exuberance that Scribner's took the book. I hope for all your sakes that it exhausts one edition. Strange, but I doubted that you would like it, why, I don't know. And when I sent it I did not believe that you intended to do anything with it only read it. Well, it was a surprise. The wire came early in the morning over the telephone and getting me angrily out of bed at seven—I had not planned to do anything with it for five or six more years. But while the MS was sunk my ambition was sunk also. You know how much I appreciate what you've done don't you.
>
> Love to Zelda,
> Tom (Boyd)[59]

Fitzgerald's efforts lifted Boyd out of his depression and restored his confidence. With the improvement in his professional life, his personal problems came to an end. He ended his affair with Sandra, and he and Peggy settled back into a loving relationship.

Like most young men, Thomas Boyd found his direction in life during his early twenties. Unlike most, however, Boyd experienced dramatic changes in that direction. In just three years he went from a young man on his way to a career as a cigar store manager to a literary editor, a budding socialist, and soon a published author. From 1919 to 1922, Boyd met several strong-minded and influential people, not the least of whom was his wife. He emerged at the end of 1922 as a confident man, sure of his abilities and on the verge of becoming what he had always wanted to be.

chapter four

"the best war book since The Red Badge of Courage"

SCRIBNER'S DECISION TO PUBLISH *Through the Wheat* thrust Thomas Boyd into the world of publishing authors. Within a few days, he and Peggy became St. Paul celebrities. The newspapers made much of the writing couple, running stories about Tom, Peggy, and even Betty Grace along with their photographs; and local literary clubs asked them to speak at meetings. A pair of photographs taken for publicity purposes shows the Boyds posed on the stoop of a downtown apartment building. In the better of the two pictures, Tom, dressed in a dark gray or blue suit, white shirt, and dark tie, clutching gloves and a cane in his right hand, left hand casually placed in his trousers pocket, stands two steps above, looking down at Peggy, who looks up at him. She wears a dark, heavy dress, belted at the waist and with a wide, white collar. Tom appears stiff and uncomfortable in front of the camera, while Peggy seems to be enjoying herself and Tom's discomfort. Public attention often made Boyd uncomfortable, but by the end of 1923, he had grown accustomed to it. The year would bring Boyd money and a reputation as an up-and-coming author. And his success would allow him and Peggy to fulfill a lifelong dream of traveling to Europe.

Boyd spent the first few months of 1923 revising, worrying over, and improving *Through the Wheat*. To get him started on the revisions, F. Scott Fitzgerald wrote a lengthy and specific letter of criticism that he mailed to Boyd along with the manuscript. Most of his suggestions involved advice about avoiding contractions and profanity, and corrections of misspelled words; but the letter also included more substantive changes. He suggested that Boyd delete any explanations of the main character William Hicks's personal philosophy in order to make Hicks's youth clear to the reader and, therefore, eliminate the need for any lengthy exploration of Hicks's background. In several places he changed and added words, and he rewrote a speech given by a general before a battle to soften the satire. To ease the pedagogical tone of his suggestions, Fitzgerald closed the letter by stating, "If you don't like any of these changes you can change them back on the proof."[1] Boyd, more than willing to accept the role of protégé, followed all of Fitzgerald's suggested changes.

Naturally, Max Perkins, Boyd's editor at Scribner's, played the most important editorial part in the preparation of *Through the Wheat*. Perkins liked the book in its original form, and his guiding principle in editing it was to leave it the way it was when he first saw it. He felt that the simple and uneven nature of *Through the Wheat* added to its effect. Most of his editorial efforts, apart from standard grammatical and structural changes, involved fending off Boyd's suggestions for changes. He made several, including inserting numbers between the sections within chapters and wrapping the book in a bright yellow book jacket. These ideas and others that Perkins deemed unwise were politely squelched. Perkins was determined to defend the integrity of the manuscript from any suggestion of pretension and sophistication.[2]

The only part of the book that worried Perkins was the ending. Unsure of his reading, he asked his cousin, Richard Evarts, to read *Through the Wheat* and give his opinion. When Evarts agreed that the final scene of the book left the reader confused about the main character's physical location and mental state, Perkins wrote Boyd and asked him to make the conclusion more definitive.[3] In the final scene of the novel, Hicks wanders in front of the enemy lines, exposing himself to enemy fire while searching for his machine gun, oblivious to the danger. The scene has a surreal feel and Boyd's phrasing is somewhat abstract. He intended to convey that Hicks had become inured to his surroundings, the suffering of others, and the idea that he might be killed. Without forcing the issue, Boyd wanted to communicate the effect of modern warfare on the men who fought, and he resisted any wholesale changes. He protested that he could think of nothing significant to add or subtract but changed the last line to "Hicks was exalted: Gethsemanied."[4] Later he changed the line again, to "Hicks was exalted: lost in the absolute." Finally, he settled on the simpler "The soul of Hicks was numb." Perkins liked this last change best, and it would appear as the last line of the book; but he continued to lobby, unsuccessfully, for Boyd to change it in later editions.[5]

Perkins quickly put the book into proofs and sent them to Boyd on January 23, 1923. He made few suggestions on the proofs; and as he intended, *Through the Wheat* went to press in much the same form as he had first read it. Most of the correspondence between Perkins and Boyd centered on Perkins's promotional ideas. He felt that along with the standard literary critics, *Through the Wheat* should be reviewed by enlisted men who had served during the war. He hoped veterans would provide Scribner's with blurbs that could be used in advertising copy promoting the book. As the publication date approached, Perkins asked Boyd for a list of veterans who might be willing to provide favorable statements. He responded with a list that did not completely meet Perkins's needs but did include Major General John A. Lejuene, the commandant of the United States Marine Corps; Colonel Albertus Catlin; Dan Daly, the most decorated American soldier during the war; John A. McEwan, Peggy's cousin and the West Point football coach; and Reed Landis, a veteran and acquaintance of Tom's from Chicago and the son of baseball commissioner Kenesaw Mountain Landis. Boyd also requested that Perkins send review copies to Amy Lowell and Theodore Dreiser. Perkins complied with Boyd's wishes, but he also sought out other veterans to review the book.[6] Most servicemen responded positively to the frank and accurate depictions of combat in *Through the Wheat*, and Perkins gleaned ad copy from the best of their responses. At Tom's suggestion, he also contacted the U.S. Marines publicity bureau in Washington, D.C., in the hopes of receiving some official response, though he doubted it would be positive.[7]

Perkins did not ignore the more traditional reviewers. On April 3, he mailed a barrage of letters to critics including Edmund Wilson, Heywood Broun, and Robert Sherwood in an attempt to generate favorable prepublication buzz about *Through the Wheat*. His letter to Wilson was typical:

> I am sending you an advance copy of "Through the Wheat" by Thomas Boyd—a war book. For one thing, you yourself wrote what I remember as vividly as when I stopped reading, the best piece of war fiction I ever saw in "Death of a Soldier." And for another, Fitzgerald said you ought to have an advanced copy and would be interested in it.[8]

As the April 27 publication date approached, Perkins continued to refine the manuscript up until the last moment, writing to Boyd on the twenty-fourth to ask if he had used a military term in the proper context.[9] A rising star at Scribner's, Perkins had staked some part of his reputation on the success of *Through the Wheat*.[10] Fortunately for both Perkins and Boyd, the book did succeed.

Critical praise for *Through the Wheat*, both that of professional critics and that of amateurs, was almost universally positive. Not surprisingly, Fitzgerald lavished praise on the novel in his review that appeared in the *New York Evening Post Literary Review:*

> There are no treasured up reactions to aesthetic phenomena poured along the pages, either for sweetening purposes or to endow the innately terrible with a higher relief. The whole book is written in the light of one sharp emotion and hence it is as a work of art rather

> than as a text book for patrioteer or pacifist that the book is arresting. . . . To my mind, this is not only the best combatant story of the great war, but also the best war book since "The Red Badge of Courage."[11]

Other reviewers and authors who had no interest in the success of Boyd or his novel also heaped accolades on both. In a personal letter to Boyd, Theodore Dreiser wrote:

> I have just finished "Through the Wheat." With the exception of Latzko's "Men in War" and Crane's "Red Badge of Courage" I do not recall a war book that has so gripped and moved me. The sense of duty, of compulsion, of chance, of lunacy, of decency, of courage, of honor, of dignity, of shame—it's all here. You have written a fine book and I wish for it and you every thing you wish for it and for yourself. My compliments and regard.[12]

Published reviews were also laudatory. The *Nation* called *Through the Wheat* "a remarkable first novel."[13] Edmund Wilson, writing for the *Dial*, concluded, "This is probably the only candid account on record of what it meant to be a hero in the Marines and a valuable document on the ordinary human virtues in reaction to the conditions of modern warfare."[14] And the reviewer for the *New York Times* wrote, "After the tornado of war books has swept by . . . and after the black clouds have blown away, it has remained for Thomas Boyd to write the least partisan and the most brilliant of the doughboy reminiscences."[15] *Through the Wheat* was a critical success, as most of the serious critics praised its honesty and its simplicity.

Not all those who read *Through the Wheat* liked the book. Deputy General Brent G. Nunnaly of the Kentucky American Legion wrote a long letter condemning the book:

> On April 20th you mailed me a complimentary copy of Thomas Boyd's book "Through the Wheat." Perhaps I am not qualified to

> criticize literary work of any kind but in my honest and humble opinion this book is absolutely rotten.
>
> In the first place, it very emphatically states from cover to cover that the leadership entrusted to the American Army officers was a farce and that the system of the United States Army was a joke.
>
> In the second place, I believe in plain speech and freedom of the press, but I see no reason why we should perpetuate and hand down to future generations a book couched in so undignified and common language as the author used in this book even though it be true. We all know that men did things and said things during the war that today they want to forget.
>
> Personally, I think the greater failure of this book, the greater the chances of success will be ours in teaching Americanism to Americans.[16]

Nunnaly's opinion mirrored the ideas and goals of the officers and rear-echelon personnel that Boyd ridiculed in *Through the Wheat*. Soldiers and officers who saw a great deal of the front-line fighting praised the book or at the very least found nothing offensive or dangerous. Marine General Logan Feland, one of Boyd's commanding officers, wrote, "I was so glad in reading your 'Through the Wheat' that the harangue by a fat general before we went into the Argonne influenced you in the ranks exactly as it did me at the head of the Regiment. But you are out and can say it while I am in and cannot."[17] Lieutenant Colonel John Hughes (known to the marines he commanded as Johnny the Hard) willingly and even enthusiastically agreed to promote the book at the reunion of the 2nd Division scheduled for July.[18]

With the critical reception of *Through the Wheat* assured, Perkins and Boyd waited for news of its sales. Perkins tried to prepare Boyd for poor sales figures. "This business is full of disappointments so you must not count on much yet, but you are certainly entitled to feel exceedingly gratified by the way the book has been received, and we are certainly proud to be its publisher."[19] Happily for both men, the book was a limited public success. By June 11, Scribner's had ordered a second printing and sales were climbing.[20]

At the end of the month, orders from bookshops had reached 8,000 and by mid-July, actual sales had reached 5,000 copies.[21] Sales continued to mount through the summer, reaching their peak in August when *Through the Wheat* was at the top of the *Chicago Tribune*'s bestseller list. A year later the book would be in its seventh printing.

The book was a sensation in St. Paul, making Boyd a minor local celebrity. A few days after *Through the Wheat* was published, Boyd wrote Perkins complaining that the furor it had caused at Kilmarnock Books had kept him from writing.[22] And writing was what Boyd wanted to do now more than ever. The success of his first novel convinced him that he could make a living as a writer and he never wanted to do anything else.

Peggy Boyd was pregnant for much of 1923. The pregnancy severely hampered her writing. She had begun a second novel almost as soon as *The Love Legend* hit the shelves and throughout the spring and summer of 1923 she worked on it when she could. But her ultimately tragic second pregnancy made her very ill and prevented her from working steadily.[23] She finally completed the manuscript for her second novel, *Lazy Laughter,* during the summer of 1923. Scribner's accepted it on August 6, 1923.[24] Based on the strength and promise of *The Love Legend,* Peggy received a $375 advance and the book was slated for fall publication.[25] Like Peggy's first novel, *Lazy Laughter* was the story of an independent modern girl, Dagmar, determined not to fall into the trap of an unfulfilling marriage and boring life. When the novel was published in November 1923, the critics responded kindly but not effusively. The *New York Tribune* review was typical. "'Lazy Laughter' holds more of promise than of performance but it is distinctly interesting in both ways."[26] The reviewer for the *Cleveland Plain Dealer* was equally tepid: "When the effect of the book as a whole takes possession of the reader there comes the conviction that quietly and by subtle means the author has done an acute and not at all superficial satire."[27] Perhaps damned by faint praise, *Lazy Laughter* failed to sell. By February 1924 the meager sales it generated had completely dried up.[28]

During the last months of 1922 and the first months of 1923 Boyd had begun writing a new novel with the working title "The Duke Rides Past."

The manuscript's central figure was a girl named Heloise Leslie who is forced to marry against her will and against her passion. Boyd, nervous of the reception it would receive from Scribner's, hesitated before sending it to Perkins. In one letter he compared writing a girl's story to "crossing a stream on an elm tree (felled) after the rain."[29] He held the manuscript, refining and polishing the story and the prose, until the middle of September and hoped that if Perkins thought it worthy, it could be serialized in a magazine to maximize the earnings he would receive.[30] Unfortunately, despite Boyd's care, Perkins felt that it was not the right novel to follow *Through the Wheat* and encouraged him not to push for publication.[31] Boyd took the news of the rejection well, responding only that he would continue to work on the "The Duke Rides Past" and that "when I have little to write, I can go back to it with a fresh point of view."[32] He never found a time when he had "little to write," and neither Scribner's nor any other publisher ever published "The Duke Rides Past."

Part of the reason for Boyd's casual reaction to the rejection of "The Duke Rides Past" may have been that he had already begun another novel-length writing project in the summer of 1923. He first mentioned the new novel to Perkins in August 1923.[33] He had already written much, given the novel the title *The Dark Cloud*, and confidently predicted that he would have it completed in three weeks.[34] Circumstances and other writing projects prevented him from keeping to his time schedule.

In addition to the work he put in on two novels, Boyd began writing short stories, which he sent to Perkins for his opinion and so that Perkins could act as a go-between with Robert Bridges, the editor of *Scribner's* magazine. For the remainder of 1923 and into 1924, Perkins would help Boyd improve the stories, select the right ones for magazine publication, and put them in the order he thought would have the most positive effect. Max Perkins liked to follow a successful novel with a book of short stories and was already making plans for a book of Boyd's stories.

Convinced of their ability to support themselves as writers and eager to begin enjoying the lifestyle of successful authors, Tom and Peggy Boyd planned an extended vacation in France. They had no pretensions about joining the American expatriate community in Paris but had dreamed of taking a long trip through Europe even before they were married. Boyd's earnings from *Through the Wheat* made it possible.[35]

Beginning their journey in mid-September 1923, the Boyds planned a leisurely trip across the country, stopping in Chicago to leave their daughter Betty Grace with Peggy's parents and in Cleveland to visit Alice Boyd, and then on to New York where they would meet and mingle with the New York literati. They had booked passage on a ship leaving for France in late November.[36]

The trip began badly. Boyd had a miserable time in Chicago. Though the Chicago papers ran pictures of Tom, Peggy, and Betty Grace and they were treated as visiting authors of high reputation, Boyd found much about which to be unhappy. He caused a scene at a local bookstore when they had no copies of *Through the Wheat* on display. He found Peggy's ex-roommate Rose Caylor very irritating, feeling she played at being an author, and he claimed that he would rather spend a week in hell than in Chicago. His mood improved once they were on the train for Cleveland. The view of the Ohio landscape rolling by outside the train window restored Boyd's spirits. In Cleveland they were treated like celebrities by the local press and the mayor, and no record of any tension related to their stay with Tom's mother exists.

Their arrival in New York prompted little fanfare. They spent most of their time visiting their friends and making new literary acquaintances. The Fitzgeralds entertained them at their home in Great Neck on Long Island, where they met Ring Lardner. Tom, Scott, and Lardner spent most of one day getting drunk and talking. The Boyds then spent a week with Max Perkins in Plainfield, New Jersey, where they got a taste of country club life, played whist, and saw a polo match. The rest of their stay was spent at the Ambassador Hotel, hobnobbing with many of New York's up-and-coming writers. They met Charles MacArthur, whom Peggy had known in Chicago, and had lunch at the Algonquin Round Table at the invitation of Thyra Winslow.[37]

The Boyds boarded ship for France on November 18, 1923. They planned an extended stay in the south of France, followed by a working tour of

World War I battlefields and a walking tour of the Welsh and English countrysides. Boyd's intention was to support himself and Peggy in Europe through writing, and he planned to complete several stories and the manuscript for *The Dark Cloud* while living in France. Their trip, begun in joy and anticipation, ended in disappointment.

The Boyds arrived at Cherbourg, France, near the end of November 1923 and moved quickly inland to Caen, where they spent a weekend before moving to Paris. There they took up residence at the Hôtel de L'Intendance on the rue d'Université. Boyd had been seasick during the trip across the Atlantic, but he enjoyed the beauty of the green grass and old buildings of Cherbourg and Caen. Paris proved disappointing. Peggy became ill and complained of the cold.[38] For Boyd, Paris held little of the appeal felt by American expatriates. They stayed only a week, and no record exists of any contact with famous Americans living in Paris at the time. In a letter to Max Perkins written just before they left Paris, Boyd shared his opinion of the city and the Americans he found there with Max Perkins:

> Paris is lovely except for the queer places—Montemarte and Montparnasse the two places for poseurs—at the latter Americans pay 8 francs for a 1 franc drink and hear "Yes We Have No Bananas" (Jazz Orchestra), see still life pictures on the walls and get elbowed by ugly perspiring women because they hope to escape the curse of the bourgeoisie in that way.[39]

On November 24, Tom and Peggy boarded a train bound for Hyères, a little town on the French Riviera between Toulon and Nice. Both looked forward to the warmer climate and quieter atmosphere, and Boyd hoped to complete most of his writing projects before January 1924.[40]

Their trip to Hyères, search for a suitable place to stay, and attempts to connect with friends they made on the ship from America provided Peggy with comedic material for a letter to Elinor Merrill, whom she had met in Paris. Of the trip she wrote, "It had its ups and downs, its fumblings with the French tongue, its lights and shadows, and one purple shadow which darkened our lives only yesterday and illuminated magnificently our engaging stupidity." According to her letter, she and Tom embarked on their journey from the Gare de Lyon for Marseilles after accidentally ordering a second breakfast at the station's restaurant while trying to get two glasses of water. At Avignon a French couple got on the train and sat in the Boyds' compartment. For the rest of the trip to Marseilles they attempted to carry on a conversation without much success. The Boyds spent the night in Marseilles and then took an early train to Hyères. At the station in Hyères, they were assailed by a crowd of uniformed hotel porters who insistently offered their services and promoted their hotels. They were only dispelled when Peggy, in something of a panic, began to shout out "Maritima," the name of the hotel where they planned to stay, at which point an old man stepped forward, offered to take them to the hotel, and guided them to his horse-drawn carriage. Tom and Peggy were somewhat alarmed when the old man directed the carriage out of Hyères but soon learned that the Maritima Hôtel was located in Hyères La Plage, not Hyères itself. The Maritima itself proved to be a disappointment. The clerk showed them to a beautiful, large room with a balcony overlooking the lake; but when he quoted them a price, Tom, apparently convinced that they were being cheated, left in a huff. The Boyds walked next door to the Hôtel La Plage where they rented an almost identical room at a cheaper price.

In the confusion over the hotel and which Hyères they were looking for, the Boyds missed their rendezvous with the Wrenns, whom they had met on the ship from America. Harold Wrenn was an architect from Norfolk, Virginia, who had sold all his property and was moving his wife and two children to France so that he could study architecture. Wrenn's adventuresome decision impressed Tom, and the Wrenns and the Boyds had planned to meet in Hyères. During the first week of the Boyds' stay they had a series of near-misses with the Wrenns, which resulted in the Wrenns' decision to move on without seeing Tom and Peggy. Peggy was deeply disappointed at not having friends with them in Hyères, but Tom took advantage of the solitude to begin writing.[41]

After a few days spent getting used to their surroundings, both the Boyds began writing. Peggy eventually finished a story titled "Salon," which she sent to Perkins in January.[42] Though Perkins expressed disappointment in the story, it was eventually published in *Scribner's*.[43] Boyd embarked on one of the most productive periods of his career. He had begun writing stories for Perkins and *Scribner's* before he left for France and continued to work on them in Paris and Hyères. He completed five stories between November 1923 and February 1924. Three of them—"Rintintin," "Unadorned," and "Sound Adjutants Call"—were published by *Scribner's* in 1924. Most of the stories were completed before Christmas 1923 when Tom began to revise and rework the manuscript for *The Dark Cloud*.

The Dark Cloud is very different from *Through the Wheat* and unlike any of Boyd's other works. The story was not an original conception but rather was borrowed from the diary of a young English boy who had traveled to America as a sailor, jumped ship in Quebec, fallen in with an American abolitionist, and wandered the Ohio countryside before going to work on a Mississippi riverboat. Cornelius Van Ness had unearthed the diary in his search for lost and rare books, and Boyd had decided to rework the story as his next novel.[44] For Boyd, part of the story's appeal lay in its description of the Ohio countryside where he had grown up, but the main attraction lay in the similarities between his own childhood and the childhood of the author of the diary. Some passages from *The Dark Cloud* may reveal Boyd's feelings about his own childhood:

> Hugh Turner had never seen his father. In fact, he had not even been born until two months after Hugh Turner Senior had inconsiderately died from a pulmonary hemorrhage, leaving his young wife with little more than enough money to pay for the services of a midwife.
>
> . . . Grandfather Willard . . . after many frowning shakes of his head, numerous appeals to his Maker, and constant reminders that he had prophesied evil if Prudence ran off with that disgraceful Hugh Turner . . . packed off his daughter and grandchild. . . . The mother had returned to her parents because she had no other place to go. . . . Hugh could not help but see it: they made him feel as if he were so much more of a limb of Satan than they or any one else, perhaps excepting his dead father.[45]

Although on the surface *The Dark Cloud* appears to be an anomaly in Boyd's career, in many ways it was his most personal book. Cloaked as the character Hugh Turner, Boyd may have felt free to share his true feelings about his difficult childhood.

Boyd began work on *The Dark Cloud* in August 1923 and promised Perkins a completed manuscript in three weeks. While it is doubtful that he kept to that timeline, he was able to show Perkins at least part of the novel when he visited the New York area in the fall of 1923.[46] Before Boyd left for France, Perkins made several suggestions—adding chapter divisions, including a love interest, and publishing the book as a novel aimed at juveniles—which Boyd considered while reworking the novel in France.[47] On December 7, 1923, he wrote Perkins that he would be sending at least part of the revised manuscript of *The Dark Cloud* in six weeks.[48] Perkins urged Boyd to write well and rapidly so that the book could be in print as soon as possible.[49] On January 4, 1924, Boyd wrote to inform Perkins that he had "changed it around a good deal and sketched in a girl to help the final chapters."[50] Twelve days later he sent the nearly completed manuscript to Perkins. He apologized for the rough condition of the final chapter, saying, "I can't look at it again for a while. I'm sick over it."[51] As with *Through the Wheat*, how to end the book posed a problem for Boyd, and the ending would be one of the few problems that Perkins pointed out after reviewing the manuscript.

Despite Boyd's prodigious output and his complaint that there was very little to do in Hyères, he did not spend all his time locked away in his hotel room writing. The Boyds occasionally entertained new friends and acquaintances while living at the Hôtel La Plage. During the Christmas season of 1923, Tom and Peggy indulged in one of the few bacchanalia of their trip. On Christmas Eve they went to a party at the villa of a wealthy Frenchman, where they sang, drank, and danced with a Swiss painter and his wife and a Mr. Browne from England before returning to the hotel. There they met a Mr. and Mrs. Stevens from Columbus, Ohio, who claimed to be related to Warren G. Harding, and went out with them to eat. At a local restaurant, the Boyd party drank more wine and ordered oysters and mussels that they found inedible. Back at the hotel they found Peggy's friend Elinor Merrill, with whom they stayed up late talking and drinking.[52] On Christmas morning the Boyds and their friends gathered in their room for an American-style breakfast of bacon and eggs, after which they went swimming in the Mediterranean and consumed a bottle of scotch and a bottle of wine. After dinner that night, Douglas Gorman, a young Englishman whom Tom and Peggy had met in Paris, showed up, and the Boyds took him out and got him drunk.[53] Though not prudish, Boyd did not generally enjoy long periods of drunkenness the way other American writers seemed to: it detracted from his ability to work, and his relative sobriety perhaps helps explain his productivity.

With most of his writing projects complete, Tom and Peggy set off on what they hoped would be the first of many walking tours in Europe. They left Hyères on foot, intending to walk down the French Riviera to Nice.[54] Three days after beginning their journey, they arrived in Saint-Tropez on January 24. They had covered thirty miles and decided to stop for a day before continuing on to Nice.[55] Three days later they arrived in Nice with plans to stay at the Hôtel Beau Rivage for a week.[56] While in Nice, Peggy became quite ill. A doctor's examination revealed that she was several weeks pregnant. In light of her troubled pregnancy history, the Boyds made a hurried trip back to Paris and then on to the United States so that Peggy could be near her parents and American doctors.[57] By mid-February they were back in St. Paul.

Disappointed that they had been forced to cut their trip short, both the Boyds could nonetheless look forward to 1924 as a year in which they could continue to live the lives of young, publishing authors. The past year had produced incredible changes in their lives, and Thomas Boyd was now convinced that he could support himself and his family through writing alone. His output—two novels and six short stories—during the past twelve months indicated that he was willing to work hard to succeed as a writer and he seemed poised at the beginning of a successful publishing career.

chapter five

"It is the loveliest old farm in the world"

For all the changes brought about by the publication of Tom and Peggy Boyd's first novels—media attention, increased income, the freedom to travel abroad—the years following their return to the United States were, perhaps, the most tumultuous of their lives. Filled with professional accomplishments and disappointments as well as personal tragedy, the events of 1924 and 1925 left their mark on the Boyds. Despite their earnest attempts to establish some stability in their lives, this period would end much as had the previous years, with the Boyds scraping by and wandering the country.

The Boyds returned to St. Paul in pieces. Tom arrived ahead of Peggy, who stopped in Aurora, Illinois, for a while to rest and be with her parents. He briefly lived in the home of his friend and sometime mentor Charles Flandrau before moving all of his and Peggy's belongings to the home of another friend on St. Paul's Summit Avenue. They lived there for a week after Peggy and Betty Grace arrived and then moved into an apartment at 30 South St. Albans.[1]

Their most immediate concern was money. They had left France so quickly that Max Perkins had sent Boyd his February royalty check for $195.76 as well as a check for $200 for his story "Sound Adjutants Call" to his bank account in France.[2] The delay in redirecting the funds left the Boyds temporarily impoverished. To make matters worse, his friend and partner in Kilmarnock Books, Cornelius Van Ness, was unable to give Boyd a job. The store had caught fire while the Boyds were in France, and Van Ness had hired another man to manage the store in Boyd's absence. He would eventually return to the bookstore as something of a patron, but in the near term it offered no remedy for his financial problems. Boyd's solution to their lack of funds was to write as much and as quickly as possible.[3]

Professionally, the outlook for the coming years seemed promising. Boyd received a contract for *The Dark Cloud* shortly after returning to the United States.[4] The contract contained no provision for an advance and offered the same royalty, 10 percent, as he had been paid for *Through the Wheat*. Under ordinary circumstances this might have given Boyd little pause, but in his desperate financial circumstances he boldly asked for an advance and for the right to negotiate an independent contract for *The Dark Cloud* with an English publisher. He pointed out that Peggy had received an advance for her second novel with Scribner's, and he rather pointedly hinted that he was offended at not being offered one.[5] Perkins responded quickly, offering Boyd a five-hundred-dollar advance on the novel's earnings and apologizing for not arranging for one in the first place.[6] By the time he received Perkins's offer, he had begun to feel ashamed of his brazen demand for money. He declined the advance, saying, "I don't suppose there's much sense in having one. If the book sells it will sell and if it doesn't I certainly don't want money for it."[7] Perkins solved the Boyds' immediate monetary problems by issuing them a check equaling the amount of the two checks he had sent to France.[8] Boyd also learned that Scribner's was publishing *Through the Wheat* in England and received permission to negotiate an independent contract with an English publisher for *The Dark Cloud*. He hoped that sales in England would increase his income and further solidify his position as a successful author, but ultimately his royalties from sales in Great Britain amounted to little.[9]

The more promising source of immediate money seemed to be writing and placing short stories with literary magazines. The three stories that Boyd completed while in France had already been accepted by *Scribner's* magazine and would appear in the April, May, and July editions respectively.[10] The magazine paid Boyd two hundred dollars each for these stories, but by the time he returned to St. Paul he had spent all the money except that which he had received for "Sound Adjutant's Call."[11] He was becoming anxious about two other stories he had written and sent from Paris. The first, "Johnny the Hard," had reached Perkins, who praised it and attempted to return it to Boyd in France for corrections. Like the check, "Johnny the Hard" got lost in the intercontinental shuffle. But Perkins could not easily compensate for its loss. Convinced that it was a sure two-hundred-dollar paycheck, Boyd pursued it through various postmasters, but the story was never returned and never published.[12] The second, "Responsibility," stayed on Perkins's or magazine editor Robert Bridges's desk for some time before being accepted.[13]

After the Boyds had settled into their own apartment on St. Albans Street in early March 1924, Tom applied himself to the task of producing publishable stories while Peggy devoted herself to the health of her unborn child. "A Little Gall," the first in a series of stories written during 1924, was quickly accepted by *Scribner's*, as was Boyd's next story, "The Kentucky Boy."[14] However, his next stories failed to impress either Perkins or Bridges. Perkins returned "The Ribbon Counter" and "Our Hero" for revision so that they could be included in a collection of Boyd's short stories that Perkins planned to publish in the spring of 1925.[15] On the whole, Boyd had good luck as a short story writer during 1924. The three stories he placed with *Scribner's* earned him six hundred dollars. In addition to those three stories, he successfully placed "Uninvited" with the *Mercury* and "Semper Fidelis," a nonfiction piece, with the *Bookman*.[16] Tom and Peggy received two publishing surprises in 1924 that must have seemed like financial windfalls. Peggy received two hundred dollars for "Salon," a story written in France and initially rejected by Perkins, but then accepted for publication in *Scribner's*.[17] Then "Hawthorne and Goodwin," a story Boyd wrote with friend Hyatt Downing, also found its way into *Scribner's* and put an additional one hundred dollars in his pocket. Tom had also begun writing reviews, for which he was modestly compensated. His review of Ring Lardner's first book briefly rekindled his friendship with the author and led to more work as a reviewer.[18]

The Boyds' combined earnings for the first half of 1924 were nearly one thousand dollars. Under ordinary circumstances the money should have been enough to make ends meet. In a letter to his mother, Boyd wrote confidently of his belief in his ability to support his family through his writing, but he continued to scramble for money.[19] To help him place stories with magazines other than *Scribner's*, he hired literary agent O. K. Liverwight and asked Perkins to return the manuscripts of "The Duke Rides Past" and a long story called "Heloise" that he hoped to improve and serialize.[20] Boyd's desperate search for new sources of income was fueled by the mounting medical bills that resulted from Peggy's troubled third pregnancy.

When Peggy Boyd arrived in St. Paul in mid-February 1924, she was far from well. The pregnancy-related maladies that began in France continued in the United States and forced her to stop along the route in Aurora, Illinois, to stay with her mother before continuing to Minnesota. In a letter to his mother, Boyd alluded to the possibility of an operation for Peggy: "Peggy is not at all badly off. She gets sick sometimes and will have a more or less disagreeable time until she gets well. There is to be no operation, at least not until she is well."[21] His natural reserve, even with his mother, makes it difficult to understand the nature of Peggy's problem and the possible operation and downplays Peggy's suffering. Unable to write, rarely attempting even letters, Peggy remained ill much of the time until July 1924.

Boyd also began to show signs of the strain of Peggy's sickness and the mounting medical bills. On April 28 he shared with Max Perkins the problems that seemed to have been accumulating during the previous weeks:

> I've just passed through the most miserable weeks of my life. Everything and all at once. Mr. Bridges says he can only use six stories; a

> friend of years gets drunk and shows strong signs of sexual inversion; a man threatens to sue me for using his name; a former soldier bawls me out for what he believes to be a technical error in Rin Tin Tin [*sic*]; a YMCA man writes of the story very angrily and Mr. Bridges passed the note on to me with the request I write this man a polite note. If Mr. Bridges is not shocked with my answer to his request—well.[22]

Considering his financial situation and Bridges's support of his work, Boyd's answer is shockingly angry, blunt, and perhaps a sign that he had begun to buckle under the pressure in his personal life:

> And where are the changes which I might wish to make in Rin Tin Tin before it appears in a book? And where are the pains which my critic is supposed to have taken with the story? And why do you suggest that I write a polite note to this person who never saw the front or an enemy, who was in the Young Men's Christian Association and who apparently, with hundreds of thousands of people in America—since there are the American Magazine, Saturday Evening Post, etc.,—expect to find lies and are bitter if they do not find them? I am not Mary Raymond Shipman Andrews and thank whatever Christ there may be for that. No I shan't write a polite note, or any other kind. Had this man been a soldier I should have answered him: I cannot credit him with the alleged achievements of his ancestors.[23]

The note clearly expressed Boyd's feelings; but had circumstances been otherwise, he probably would not have written it. In addition to his feelings about the man who criticized "Rintintin," the note reveals that Boyd remained firm in his combat soldier's prejudice against rear-echelon personnel and in his frustration at not being able to place stories with high-paying and popular magazines. Perkins's advice, "A soft answer turneth away wrath," arrived too late to stop the letter, but it did not do permanent damage to his relationship with Bridges or *Scribner's*.[24]

Things were not all bad for Boyd during the spring of 1924. He received a request for a serial from *Everybody's* magazine, though it never materialized, and the *American Legion Monthly* continued to give favorable coverage to his work.[25] He received a lively letter from F. Scott Fitzgerald, who was in France living at the Grimms Park Hôtel in Hyères and planning to take advantage of the peace and quiet to write. Though Boyd's reports of the beauty and peace of Hyères undoubtedly influenced the Fitzgeralds' decision to take up residence there, Scott and Zelda lived a much more extravagant life in the south of France than had the Boyds. Supporting himself by publishing short stories, Fitzgerald arrived in Hyères with an English nurse, seventeen pieces of luggage, and plans to rent a large villa complete with a maid and a butler. He had already begun work on *The Great Gatsby* and expressed high hopes for the novel in his letter to Boyd: "Well I shall write a novel better than any novel ever written in America and become par excellence the best second rater in the world."[26]

Whatever happiness the letter brought was short-lived. On the night of June 30 Tom and Peggy's fourth child, a daughter, was born prematurely; she died on the morning of July 1. On July 2, Boyd wrote two letters, one to Perkins and one to his mother, in which he described the events of the birth. To Perkins he wrote:

> Peggy's trouble has come to a point and subsided. It was perhaps the most ghastly experience of my life. The baby, twenty-seven weeks old, arrived before the doctor or nurse. Then two doctors and a Christian Science practitioner (who has been assisting Peggy) came and towards two in the morning the nurse and I drove the baby to the incubator ward of Miller hospital. It died at six o'clock and my nerve was so gone that I had to get a friend to call the undertaker.
>
> Peggy is rapidly improving and a bath and a night's sleep has enabled me to face a mountain of bills. Thus it goes. Experience comes very hard with me.[27]

He wrote essentially the same account to his mother.[28] While both clearly show the immediate emotional impact of the event on Boyd, neither letter deals with his emotional response in depth, and both are much more about his reaction and experience than Peggy's. This emphasis may be understandable in his letter to Perkins, but a more emotional account in the letter to his mother would have been natural. More troubling is the fact that both letters seem to deal more with trivial matters than with the death of his fourth child. In the letter to Perkins, he devotes more space to news about the bookstore, Ring Lardner's new book, the illustration that accompanied one of his stories in *Scribner's,* and Charly Bayley's new job with Henry Holt. Similarly, in the letter to his mother, Boyd devotes a whole paragraph to a birthday cake his mother had sent him, and he wrote at length about his publishing prospects.[29] Both letters leave the reader with the impression that Thomas Boyd was a cold, self-centered man.

However, before judging Boyd too harshly, it is important to remember several important facts of his life. At the time he wrote the letters, he was one day removed from his twenty-sixth birthday, and in his twenty-six years he had seen more death and experienced more unhappiness than most people his age. His father died before he was born, and he had been essentially abandoned by a laudanum-addicted mother for much of his youth. During the Great War he had spent much of one year at the front killing, seeing people being killed, and narrowly escaping with his own life on two occasions. In addition, he had already lived through the stillbirth of twin sons and had personally delivered his fourth child in the absence of any medical assistance. These experiences, no doubt, made him distant and dispassionate, and if they do not totally excuse his apparent callousness in the face of the death of his fourth child, they at least make it more understandable.

The medical bills and the expense of burying his daughter left Boyd deeper in debt and in need of steady income. He proposed creating and editing a book page to the publishers of the *Minneapolis Journal,* and failing that he planned to look for a job in advertising. He still believed that he could eventually support himself through writing: "At any rate it will be but a makeshift job because my principal interest is in writing books. . . . If the Dark Cloud [*sic*] sells as well as I believe it will I will have money enough to keep me."[30]

Clearly, Boyd hoped for and counted on high sales and good critical reaction to *The Dark Cloud*. Unfortunately, he would be disappointed on both counts. Scribner's published the novel in early September 1924, and Boyd waited for news of its success. Perkins, much more knowledgeable about the market for books, wrote to him to prepare him for bad news:

> We printed three thousand for a first edition and have printed another thousand. But you must prepare yourself for one thing,—you are in the difficult position of having made, at least from a literary standpoint, a great hit with your first book. This means that the second book is unlikely to be reviewed upon its merits. It is to be reviewed by an unfair standard, far more critically than a book usually is. Not only that: the background of a marked success seems somehow to have the psychological effect of prejudicing the general reviewer.[31]

Whether Perkins had received advance warnings of the book's reception or had simply divined the truth from his knowledge of the publishing business, his predictions about the reviews of *The Dark Cloud* proved accurate.

With the exception of Ruth Peter, writing for the *New York Times Magazine*, who compared *The Dark Cloud* favorably to the work of Mark Twain, most critics reviewed the book as Perkins had predicted. The review in the *New York Times Book Review* stated:

> [If] Mr. Boyd intended a wistful tragedy of egoism, he has been deflected from his purpose by the incompletely visualized task of selecting and assembling the component parts of his present—the period just before the Civil War. . . . It is to be hoped that "The Dark Cloud" is merely a transition to that splendor of creation which "Through the Wheat" eloquently foretold.[32]

John Farrar, who as editor of the *Bookman* solicited reviews and work from Boyd, expressed his disappointment with *The Dark Cloud* in his review.

> I want you to read "The Dark Cloud," but I can't help being disappointed in it. Thomas Boyd's "Through the Wheat" was a passionate and vigorous book. "The Dark Cloud" contains passages of prose so sparse as almost to be dull. Yet there is no question that Boyd is one of the best of our young writers. Perhaps he will find again the touch of genius that lifted his first book so high above the level of the usual.[33]

Stung by the critical reception of *The Dark Cloud,* Boyd wrote Perkins, "Well it was honest and, excepting for one or two passages, I am not ashamed. So what the hell."[34]

F. Scott Fitzgerald attempted to buoy Boyd's spirits with a letter he wrote after receiving an autographed copy of *The Dark Cloud*.

> I like the book enormously. First I'll say that. Not quite as well as the first because the style bothered me. Its not as simple as the first. . . .
>
> On the other hand its far bigger feat of imagination—something quite new & more in line with a big development. You might have been a one bookman and written the other, but in this you show you have the novelists temperament. . . . [35]

Whatever salve Fitzgerald's letter might have applied to the wounds Boyd received from the critics, it would not solve his financial problems if *The Dark Cloud* failed to sell.

From a commercial standpoint, *The Dark Cloud* started well. On October 20, Perkins placed the number of copies sold at around 2,600.[36] A few weeks later he reported Boyd's royalties on the sale of both *The Dark Cloud* and *Through the Wheat* as $562, which was not due to be paid until February.[37] *The Dark Cloud* sold for two dollars a copy and Boyd received 10 percent on each sale, which means that his earnings from his second novel accounted for $520 at the end of October. When Scribner's reported Boyd's February royalties, the total came to $683, which indicates that *The Dark*

Cloud sold fewer than one thousand copies between the end of October and the beginning of February.[38] In a letter written shortly after receiving the royalty report, Boyd indicated that by his calculations Scribner's was left with 1,200 copies of *The Dark Cloud*. Ultimately, the novel sold fewer than three thousand copies in the United States; and though it was published in England by Fisher Unwin, Boyd never realized the income from the book for which he had hoped.[39]

As always, Boyd had been writing during the period surrounding the publication of *The Dark Cloud*. He had begun a new novel and had typically high hopes for it. The subject of the book was the life of an Ohio farmer between 1850 and 1880.[40] Boyd intended to draw heavily on his family history and planned to move to the Ohio countryside when the lease at their St. Albans address ran out at the end of August.[41] The low returns from the sale of *The Dark Cloud* left the Boyds financially short. When Boyd got a job writing a books column for the *Minneapolis Journal*, they decided to postpone their move to Ohio and stay on in Minnesota for a few more months. At the end of August they moved to a third-story flat atop a private home at 529 Portland Avenue in St. Paul. Despite the distractions of moving, Boyd reported to Perkins that he had completed ten chapters of the new book and promised to send a few of them once he had had the chance to revise them.[42] Perkins would not actually see any part of the novel until early 1925.

Several things slowed Boyd's progress on the novel. His new home proved to be a limitation. Reachable only by stairs in the back of the house, the Portland Avenue apartment had walls and floors so thin that Tom and Peggy could not type at night for fear of raising complaints from their landlady, who lived below them.[43] In addition, Boyd's conception of the novel changed as he worked on it. Initially conceived as a single volume, it had become a trilogy by November with the tentative titles "Background," "Middle Distance," and "Foreground."[44] An unexpected visit to the Twin Cities by Sinclair Lewis cost Boyd a whole week near the end of August.

> Sinclair Lewis has been spending a week here and in consequence I haven't been to bed a single night before three o'clock. Everybody

> drank too much and while we only gave a picnic and a dinner the visit nearly wrecked me. Not only that it took a week away from the writing of the novel. . . . I like him greatly, but his vehemence and vitality nearly wore poor Peggy to a shred.[45]

Boyd was also producing a weekly column for the *Minneapolis Journal,* a task he referred to as a "hellish bother."[46] These factors, combined with the normal distractions of everyday living, made it difficult for Boyd to work consistently on the Ohio novel.

But the biggest delays to his work on the novel came from his other writing project during the fall and winter of 1924. Perkins had planned a volume of short stories for publication in the spring of 1925, and Boyd spent a good deal of time preparing material for the book. He wrote or corrected three new stories—"The Nine Days Kitten," "The Ribbon Counter," and "The Long Shot"—and sent them to Perkins for inclusion in the book. In addition, Perkins decided that the book should include an introduction for the stories.

> It also occurred to me that it might be interesting if you felt inclined, to put in a foreword in which you would tell what your purpose was in these stories. In connection with these stories and with "Through the Wheat" varying opinions have been expressed as to whether the truth was as you saw it or not. You have had letters from soldiers and others. I think if you felt like it—if you felt you had something to say—that you might give the book additional point and greater unity, by reviewing the whole matter of what you had aimed to do and of any impressions you had got about the general public attitude on account of these writings.[47]

Boyd followed through on Perkins' suggestions and wrote an introduction that fit Perkins's description very neatly.

The distractions in Boyd's life kept him from working on the Ohio novel throughout November and much of December 1924, and he put off any serious writing until after the holidays. On January 6, he wrote Perkins that he was anxious to get the short story collection, titled *Points of Honor,* through the proof stage so that he could return to work on the novel.[48] Nine days later he was finishing up the last chapter, readying himself for rewriting, and planning the trip to Ohio that he had postponed the previous summer.[49] In the interim between his work on the novel in August 1924 and January 1925 the novel had shrunk from a trilogy to a single volume.

Perkins and F. Scott Fitzgerald exchanged letters regarding Boyd's new novel that revealed much about their opinions of him and his work. In December Fitzgerald wrote, "Poor Tom Boyd! His cycle [referring to the planned trilogy] sounded so sad to me—perhaps it will be wonderful but it sounds to me like sloughing in a field whose first freshness has gone."[50] Perkins's response included his judgments of Boyd's writing abilities:

> . . . while I hardly took seriously his idea of writing a trilogy, I have hopes of the book he is now doing by itself, not because I know much of it but because I believe in him once he gets control of himself. Some of the best find that the hardest. I think he is utterly honest and has strong deep feeling, which is the greatest thing. He does not work hard over his writing—once it's down on paper it seems to bore him; but this he realizes.[51]

Fitzgerald's letter alluded to his displeasure with Boyd's new subject matter that would later blossom into anger at Boyd himself. Perkins's letter shows how accurately he understood Boyd. After only two years of working with him, Perkins had evaluated his strengths and his weaknesses as an author, and in the future he intended to do all he could to avoid a repeat of the disappointment caused by *The Dark Cloud.*

Boyd's February royalty check totaled $682, a good deal more than he had expected, with sales of *Through the Wheat* constituting much of the surprise. The Ohio novel, now titled *Samuel Drummond,* was complete, and Tom and Peggy set off on their trip to the Ohio countryside. Their first stop was Oak Park, Illinois, where they planned to stay with Peggy's parents for ten days while Peggy's mother read the manuscript; then they planned to move on to Defiance, Ohio.[52] Boyd intended the trip as a fact-finding mission to improve the authenticity of *Samuel Drummond.* Like most of his writing, the new novel had a strong personal connection—it was the story of his Grandfather Dunbar's life—and he wanted to check his descriptions of places and events against reality.

Perkins's chief concern about the new novel was Boyd's record of lackadaisical revision. In early February, before ever seeing *Samuel Drummond,* he cautioned Boyd to be careful with the rewrite. On February 9, he reported that the rewriting was going well; and in response to Perkins's admonishments about revisions he promised, "Yes, I'll try to be careful in rewriting—it's hateful work of course."[53] By March 9, Tom and Peggy had landed on the farm of his uncle in Jewell, Ohio. The manuscript was in terrible shape and there was no typewriter available to improve it; so Boyd, who had once been chastised by Perkins for sending in messy manuscripts, hesitated to send it.[54] Perkins, anxious to see the novel as soon as possible, urged him to submit it regardless of its condition.[55]

While researching *Samuel Drummond,* Tom and Peggy located and visited the house built by their common ancestor William Rohn, who was buried along with other relatives in a small family cemetery behind the home. They decided to buy the house:

> It is the loveliest old farm in the world—a hundred year old house—black walnut floors and wainscoting—*handmade*—but it has gone out of the family. We can buy it for $88,000 [$8,800]—probably less. At any rate, we shall offer $7,800 and if we get it we will have to mortgage it—pay the interest and yet improve the old place. We've simply got to do it. I refuse to live elsewhere.[56]

Boyd asked Perkins for a five-hundred-dollar advance on *Samuel Drummond.*[57] Perkins warned Tom that settling so far from an urban area would affect his ability to communicate with Scribner's and other publishers, but sent the money.[58]

Perkins need not have worried. Negotiations between Boyd and the owner of the farm were not going well; Tom and Peggy's offer remained several hundred dollars below what the owner was asking.[59] On March 20, Peggy wrote Perkins and reported on the state of their attempt to buy the house:

> The affair is still hanging fire—we pulled all our available funds together and offered to buy it from the owner—who after a great deal of dickering agreed to our price. . . . Then we discovered that there were two mortgages on it which had to be looked into—and the result of our inquiry made us back down a little. We may be running our heads into a noose.[60]

In the end the complications and expense of buying the farm prevented Tom and Peggy from returning it to family ownership. They had, however, decided not to return to Minnesota and began to look elsewhere for a new home.

Scribner's published the short story collection *Points of Honor* in March 1925. Reviews were positive. The critic who reviewed the book for the *New York Times* wrote:

> Thomas Boyd has further chronicled the adventures of the American Legions in France. To his new stories of American soldiers he brings the same competent craftsmanship and balanced point of view, and excellence of characterization that so easily distinguished his first novel.[61]

The review in the *Nation* focused on the honesty and accuracy of the stories:

> One of the most baffling questions left by such war chronicles as "Points of Honor" is whether these soldiers-authors might not go into battle again if a second holocaust arose. Despite the passion and agony that tears through each of the tales in this book, they are

> told in a voice bereft of emotion or expression—facts, simple unadorned episodes of war—but they smile with utter conviction.[62]

Despite his negative statements about Boyd's plans for *Samuel Drummond*, Fitzgerald praised *Points of Honor:* "I wrote you that I was crazy about *Points of Honor.* Since then I have read both [*Points of Honor* and *Through the Wheat*] over . . . and I think they are about my favorite modern books."[63] Clearly, Fitzgerald felt that Boyd should limit himself to writing about the war if he wished to be successful. Boyd's decision to begin writing about Ohio subjects would contribute to the split between him and Fitzgerald.

Many of the stories contained in *Points of Honor* had already been published in *Scribner's* magazine. Others had been submitted to *Scribner's* but rejected for individual publication. Two other stories were published in other magazines. The stories, taken as a whole, are in the same vein as *Through the Wheat* but, because they are less autobiographical, they offered a more varied glimpse into the experiences of American soldiers during the First World War. Some of the stories—"The Uninvited" and "The Kentucky Boy"—are quite good, but too many were forgettable.

Though *Points of Honor* won critical praise, like most short story books it enjoyed only modest sales. Only 1,495 copies had been sold by August 1925. Few reviewers or readers—other than Fitzgerald, who called it "faintly pretentious"[64]—commented on the introduction that Boyd had written at Perkins's request. From an historical perspective the introduction is important because it constitutes the first political statement Boyd ever published.

> And incidentally these stories may serve to correct the impression that I, as an author, hate war. That would not be my business. But it is my business not to glorify it; it is my business to perceive it truthfully and to set down these perceptions in such a way that they may be shared by whoever is kind enough to read them. Hate war! Hate the ambitious who cause the wars and the financiers who grow fat on them. Hate the people who believe sleek lies. If we must hate let us hate causes; it is futile to hate effects.[65]

Pretentious or not, the introduction contained the germ of Boyd's rough socialist political beliefs that many of the world's problems were caused by those with massive wealth and those who blindly followed the financially and politically powerful.

The shabby manuscript of *Samuel Drummond* arrived on Max Perkins's desk on March 24, 1925.[66] He must have taken it home and read it in its entirety that night. The next day he wrote Boyd:

> Let me say instantly that "Samuel Drummond" represents a long march forward. A book of large dimensions it is, firmly based upon everlasting verities. It accumulates power by its progress and comes, I think, to a perfect end. The greatest quality it has, to my mind, is that strong feeling for nature that you seem able to impart by some simple means of your own. . . .
>
> I can say all this,—cannot in fact refrain from saying it, and yet I ask you,—can you not put a month more work upon it. . . . I'll immediately send you a list of comments.[67]

Perkins's enthusiasm for *Samuel Drummond* was sincere. In a letter to Fitzgerald he referred to it as "a splendid piece of work" and would defend it against Fitzgerald's later attacks.[68] But just as sincere was his desire that Boyd work hard correcting and rewriting parts of the manuscript.

Boyd expressed an eagerness to get Perkins's "suggestions, corrections, emendations, and elisions." Perkins must have felt that, for once, Boyd was serious about revising his work.[69] On April 7, Perkins mailed a lengthy letter that gave an overview of what he felt were *Samuel Drummond*'s strengths and weaknesses and enclosed a list of thirty detailed notes on specific items that he felt should be corrected. The notes ranged from general pedantic admonishments like "much used phrases ought to be avoided" and "I'd never use the passive voice where you can use the shorter more direct and vivid active" to suggestions for revising whole scenes and changing plot devices.[70] Max Perkins was determined that *Samuel Drummond* would not fail due to a lack of authorial diligence and had decided to take a more active role in the preparation of Boyd's third novel. But by the time Boyd received

Perkins's notes, his enthusiasm for revision had waned. After only a few days' work he wrote, "At this stage I can do nothing more on *Samuel Drummond*. I hope you will like the changes I've made."[71] The changes did satisfy Perkins, at least temporarily; but he warned Boyd that he would have to read the proofs carefully to correct any lingering errors or confusing passages.[72]

Before the end of April the Boyds, having given up the idea of buying the farmhouse in Ohio, were once again on the move. They stopped in Cleveland and stayed with Tom's mother for ten days before heading further east and eventually settling in Vermont. They rented a large brick house overlooking the Kedron River in South Woodstock on the first of June and planned to settle there until fall.[73]

Scribner's issued a contract for *Samuel Drummond* that included an increase in royalties to 15 percent with plans to publish the novel in late summer 1925. The novel tells the story of the life of an Ohio farmer from youth through old age, following him through the establishment of his own farm, the accumulation of debt related to the purchase of modern equipment to make up for the lack of sons to help him work the farm, service in the Civil War, and the loss of his farm. With this novel Boyd had, consciously or not, moved on to the next phase of his writing career, a phase which saw him shift the focus of his work from the war to Ohio subjects.

Boyd's decision to write about Ohio subjects contributed to the loss of F. Scott Fitzgerald's support. As early as February, Fitzgerald had voiced his disappointment at Boyd's decision to write a novel like *Samuel Drummond*. In a letter written from his Paris apartment Fitzgerald wrote:

> I am anxiously awaiting *Samuel Drummond*—of course in choosing a field that so many men & women from Zola to Hardy to Sheila Kay Smith have tilled you set yourself a problem—that is you must bring twice as much freshness, data, and communicable emotion to make it absorbing.[74]

Fitzgerald disliked novels that attempted to glorify the American farmer, feeling that these sorts of books were highly derivative of works already published. In a portion of his notebook published posthumously in *The Crack-Up*, Fitzgerald satirized these novels and their authors:

> *The Barnyard Boys or Fun on the Soil:*
> George Barnyard
> Thomas Barnyard
> Glenway Barnyard
> Ladislas Barnyard, their uncle
> Knut Barnyard, their father
> Burton Smalltown, the hired man
> Chambers, a city dude
> Ruth Kitchen
> Martha Kitchen
> Willa Kitchen, their mother
> Little Edna, an Orphan
> Margaret Kitchen
>
> "How Hamsun you are looking," cried the fan.
>
> Chambers dressed 1903
>
> It was winter, summer, spring, anything you like, and the Barnyard Boys were merrily at work getting together epics of the American soil in time for the next publishing season. All day long they dug around in the great Hardy fields, taking what would come in handy.[75]

Fitzgerald's scorn for "epics of the American soil" was undisguised in his private notebooks. He felt evident disdain for novelists like Glenway Westcott and Edna Ferber, who wrote such works, which he felt were cheap imitations of Thomas Hardy or more recently of Willa Cather or Knut Hamsun. This is the type of novel that he felt Tom was writing, and the "Thomas Barnyard" in the satire is almost certainly a reference to Boyd.

By the time he wrote the letter cautioning Boyd about the problems of writing novels about farmers, Fitzgerald had either read the galleys of *Samuel Drummond* or a detailed explanation of the novel provided by Perkins. Around June 1, Fitzgerald wrote an angry and impassioned letter to Perkins in which he attacked Boyd's writing and his character:

> As you know despite my admiration for *Through the Wheat* I haven't an enormous faith in Tom Boyd either as a personality or as an artist—as I have, say in E.E. Cummings or Hemminway [*sic*]. His ignorance, his presumptuous intolerance and his careless grossness which he cultivates for vitality as a man might nurse along a dandelion with the hope that it would turn out to be an onion, have always annoyed me. . . .
>
> All this is preparatory to saying that his new book sounds utterly lousy. . . . The characters you mention have everyone, become stock-props in the last ten years—"Christy, the quaint old hired man" after a season in such stuff as Owen Davis's *Ice Bound* must be almost ready for the burlesque circuit.

Following his opening salvo, Fitzgerald launched into what he titled "The History of the Simple Inarticulate Farmer and his Hired Man Christy." He divided his history into three periods. In the first period he listed the works of George Eliot, Thomas Hardy, and Émile Zola as the originators of the characters and plots of novels about farmers and peasants and credited Hamlin Garland with writing the first American examples. Fitzgerald's second period included the works of Sheila Kay Smith, Robert Frost, Sherwood Anderson, Willa Cather, and Ruth Suckow, about whom he wrote, "These people were all good second raters (except Anderson). Each of them brought something to the business—but they exhausted the ground, the type was set. All was over." In the third period of his history he included authors whom he called "cheapskates" like Edna Ferber, Owen Davis, Glenway Westcott. He concluded his history with the all-capital satiric praise of *Samuel Drummond:* "TOM, BOYD, WRITES, NOVEL,

ABOUT, INARTICULATE, FARMER, WHO, IS, CLOSE, TO SOIL, AND, HIS, HIRED, MAN CHRISTY! 'STRONG! VITAL! REAL!'" Fitzgerald then returned to direct attacks on Boyd's character:

> I can not disassociate a man from his work—that this Westcott (who is an effeminate Oxford fairy) and Tom Boyd and Burton Rascoe (whose real ambition is to lock themselves into a stinking little apartment and screw each other's wives) are going to tell us mere superficial "craftsmen" like Hergeshiemer, Wharton, Tarkington and me about the Great Beautiful Appreciation they have of the Great Beautiful life of the Manure Widder—rather turns my stomach. The real people like Gertrude Stein . . . and Conrad . . . have a respect for people whose materials may not touch theirs *at a single point*. But the fourth rate + highly derivative people like Tom are loud in their outcry against any subject matter that doesn't come out of the old, old, bag which their betters have used and thrown away.[76]

Certainly, Fitzgerald would have been disappointed with Boyd's decision to write a novel that placed him among a group of authors for whom Fitzgerald had little respect. This disappointment helps explain Fitzgerald's opinion of *Samuel Drummond*. But it does not explain the vicious personal attacks.

The real source of Fitzgerald's rage had much more to do with *The Great Gatsby* than with *Samuel Drummond*. Fitzgerald had spent a good deal of time working on *The Great Gatsby*, and it is clear from his letter to Boyd in 1924 that he expected it to make his name in the world of serious writers. But when the book was published in the spring of 1925, it received only middling praise while books like Edna Ferber's *So Big*, which won the Pulitzer Prize that year, and Glenway Westcott's *The Apple of the Eye*, published the year before, received critical approval. So when Fitzgerald learned that Boyd was also disappointed with *The Great Gatsby*, his anger boiled over. His letter acknowledging Boyd's opinion gives no hint of his anger:

"Sorry you didn't like Gatsby—and thank you for being so nice about concealing the fact (I mean this); I think you're wrong, but time will tell."[77] But in the letter to Perkins he gave full vent to his anger at Boyd's opinion. His references to Boyd's "ignorance," "presumptuousness," "intolerance," and "grossness" and his claim that Boyd's real desire lay in adultery committed in "a stinking little apartment" sound more like a description of *The Great Gatsby*'s antagonist Tom Buchanan than Tom Boyd and indicate that, in Fitzgerald's eyes, Boyd had crossed a line in their relationship. Fitzgerald thought of Boyd and most of the writers whom he had introduced to Scribner's as his protégés. He could advise and critique their work, but he would tolerate no reversal of that relationship.

Despite his anger with Boyd and his decision to sever most direct contact with him, Fitzgerald continued to keep tabs on him and even attempted to exert some influence on his career through Perkins:

> How about Tom Boyd? Is he still going to be one of the barnyard boys? Or has he got sense and decided to write about the war, or seducing married women in St. Paul, or life in a bum Kentucky military school, or something he knows about. He has no touch of genius like Hemmingway [*sic*] and Cummings but like Dos Passos he has a strong, valuable talent. He must write about the external world, as vividly and acutely and even brilliantly as he can, but let him stop there. . . . For heavens sake, Max, curb your usual (and generally sagacious) open-mindedness and don't help him to ruin his future by encouraging his stupidest ambitions. He'll turn bitter with failure.[78]

Fitzgerald knew a great deal about Thomas Boyd, and his opinions of his talent as a writer were quite astute. His judgment about Boyd's reaction to the failure of his work proved prescient. But Fitzgerald was wrong about Boyd's motivation in writing *Samuel Drummond* and about the direction of his career. That *Samuel Drummond* seemed to Fitzgerald derivative of Thomas Hardy or Knut Hamsun was an accident of Boyd's family history.

The plot of the novel followed the basic historical record of his grandfather's experiences as an Ohio farmer from his marriage to his attempts to establish a large farm outside Defiance, Ohio, to that farm's ultimate failure and his retreat to a small home in Defiance. Boyd did allow his own economic ideas to color his interpretation of the events of his grandfather's life. Drummond's failure is portrayed as the result of the tricks of an unscrupulous banker who convinces Drummond to borrow money to purchase new, expensive farm equipment. When he fails to make the payments on the equipment, he loses the farm. The problem with *Samuel Drummond* is that it can only be as exciting as the actual life of Sam Dunbar. And, while the novel contains real insight into the difficulties faced by the American farmer and displays a much greater depth of characterization than Boyd's previous novels, the story itself is occasionally dull and predictable.

In many ways the novel is a tribute to his family and his home state. Boyd filled the novel with passages containing snippets of Dunbar family history:

> At the meeting of the Maumee and the Auglaize rivers, Samuel pointed to the opposite bank and said, "Uncle Jim was born right over there." . . . "The Indians burnt the house down," Samuel went on, "and my granddaddy fought 'em from that block house right ahead of us." He motioned towards a steep rise of ground which marked the meeting of the rivers,—a sallow faced cliff with a log stockade amidst a tumult of spreading, brilliantly plumaged trees.[79]

Woven throughout the novel are descriptions of Ohio's natural beauty:

> And Defiance itself with its wide-spread elms, its brick, green shuttered houses, its steepled county court house, had an air of pleasant human habitation. But toward the west—the direction in which Samuel was slowly driving—loomed the contrast. For at the edge of the town rose a hill and beyond its crest, the brown, deeply rutted road dwindled away into a forest of great trees, deep and unending.

> Except for a few changes the northwest section of the county remained as the Indians had left it. There were the black walnuts, the oaks, the sturdy hickories, the thick, grasping brambles and underbrush with crimson berries and dull red leaves.[80]

Had Fitzgerald bothered to learn more about Boyd or asked him his reasons for writing *Samuel Drummond,* he might have learned that Boyd's motivation was quite different than he imagined. As it was, the close relationship between Thomas Boyd and F. Scott Fitzgerald came to an end.

Boyd did, however, continue to write about Ohio subjects. On July 21 he reported that he had completed three short stories all set in Ohio.[81] Two of these, "An Ohio Fable" and "Good Roads," were accepted by Robert Bridges and published in *Scribner's* magazine. Boyd received $150 for each.[82] He further supplemented his income by speaking at Middlebury College, for which he received a one-hundred-dollar honorarium.[83] Boyd also continued to write reviews and to read and evaluate the work of American authors. In an August letter to Perkins, he revealed that he had not only read the work of Ernest Hemingway but had once met him: "Thanks for letting me read the Hemmingway [*sic*] book. He is the man I spoke about: lives in Oak Park, brother of a super-Babbitt. His writing is very strong and direct and to me it is not at all arty."[84] Though he was ultimately wrong about *The Great Gatsby*, Boyd had developed a keen eye for good writing.

Boyd's August 1925 royalty report brought welcome news. *Through the Wheat* had sold an additional 355 copies and, combined with the royalties due on *Points of Honor,* brought his check to $295.[85] Peggy's royalties were far less promising. Her two books had sold a total of five copies and earned a royalty of ninety cents since February.[86] But for the first time in several years, money did not seem to concern Tom and Peggy. They were once again attempting to buy a house—this one a small house on the Quechee River, in Woodstock, Vermont—and apparently planning to settle permanently.[87]

What did concern Boyd was the critical and popular reception of *Samuel Drummond.* Scribner's published the book on August 21, 1925. On August 22 he wrote a frank and anxious letter to Perkins about his concerns:

> Samuel Drummond has not yet come though I saw the book in Woodstock where the Hampshire Bookshop of Northampton had a sale yesterday and today—they got rid of from 6 to 10 copies. Oh, how I feel like screaming: Christ! For if the damned book doesn't go I'm done for, at least I feel so—wobbly in my innards—though remarkably I also feel like writing.[88]

For all his anxiety and Perkins's care, *Samuel Drummond* proved to be another disappointment.

Reviewers did not savage *Samuel Drummond* the way Fitzgerald had, but neither did they proclaim it a great book. Though some reviews were positive, the review that appeared in the *New York Times Book Review* was typical:

> "Samuel Drummond" is an addition to the flourishing literature of the Middlewest. The book is a conscientious and, in the main, unexciting effort to paint the life of the Midwestern farmer. . . .
>
> The large public who are intrigued by novels of the farm life will find this book true to life and with greater insight than the majority of such volumes.[89]

John Farrar's review in the *Bookman* treated Boyd and *Samuel Drummond* more gently, but the point was the same: "I do not think everyone will enjoy Mr. Boyd's clipped style, his careful development, his pages which lack luminosity. . . . It is a good book and deserves success."[90]

The failure of critics to perceive what he had seen in *Samuel Drummond* frustrated Max Perkins:

> You will see that there were some who were moved to the full by "Samuel Drummond." Others seem completely to have missed its significance, but even they seem to have been disturbed by recognizing that it had a significance they did miss.[91]

More disappointing to Boyd, however, were the book's sluggish sales. Published in August, *Samuel Drummond* had sold only 2,739 copies by December and would continue to sell poorly.[92]

By the second week of October 1925, Boyd had apparently made a decision about what he needed to do to support his family. Abandoning their plans to buy the house in Woodstock, the Boyds accepted an invitation from a friend of Peggy's to spend the winter and 1925/26 living in her carriage house in Columbus, Georgia. Boyd must have begun looking for work shortly after arriving in Georgia and soon landed a job as a reporter with the *Atlanta Georgian*. The preceding two years had been unsettling, disappointing, and occasionally tragic. As the Boyds headed south, they no doubt hoped that their years in Georgia would be calmer and happier.

chapter six

"I'm better at explaining than inventing"

SHORTLY AFTER ARRIVING in Columbus, Georgia, in October 1925, Tom and Peggy Boyd took a short trip to Warm Springs. A photograph taken during the trip shows Boyd dressed in a one-piece bathing suit by a tree-lined body of water. His arms draw his knees to his chest, and his face, turned to the side toward the camera, wears an expression of anxious happiness. The years 1925 to 1929 were among the happiest and most lucrative years of Tom and Peggy Boyd's lives together. But there were currents below the surface, often masked by the trappings of success and happiness, that threatened their marriage.

The Boyds settled in Columbus on the property of a Mrs. Chappell, living first in her home, Dinglewood, and then in a small cottage on the property. Boyd described it as "a green one, with plenty of windows and shade, set far back in a yard on which there are many trees spreading over the green grass and the rather exotic shrubbery. And in a kind of thicket by one of the bedrooms you can hear and see red birds and blue jays all day long."[1]

In the weeks following their move, Tom and Peggy made the rounds of Columbus society, meeting city elders, going to clubs and dinners and to a party at Fort Benning. Boyd judged the Southerners he met rather harshly:

> We have found out a good bit about the people. They are rather agreeable, ungrammatical, prejudiced, obliging, unenlightened . . . people who remember the Civil War rather well, are contemptuous of army officers and down in their hearts do not like Northerners. . . . They do not belong to the Unites States of America and are very proud of it.[2]

Despite his negative feelings about the people, Boyd planned to remain in the South for an extended period.

Boyd would stay in the cottage he so affectionately described only a few months. In early December he moved to Atlanta. His move was prompted by his success in securing a job as a reporter for the *Atlanta Georgian*. His reasons for leaving Columbus were probably financial, but it is possible that Peggy encouraged the move because of Tom's growing familiarity with the apparently accommodating Mrs. Chappell.[3] Whatever the cause of his quick departure, the separation from Peggy brought on a surge of emotion rarely demonstrated in their relationship.

Boyd arrived in Atlanta during the first week of December 1925 and took up residence at the Henry Grady Hotel, which he described as a "traveling man's delight." The room had hot and cold running water, a shower, a bath, and a comfortable bed, but the absence of Peggy left Boyd lonely and unhappy. Though Peggy and Betty Grace joined him shortly after Christmas, which he had spent in Columbus, and though Peggy made at least one trip to Atlanta, Tom barraged Peggy with letters. Many contained passages that provide a glimpse into the depths of his feelings for her, or at least his physical longing. They are filled with professions of loneliness: "I'm pining to see you. Very much. Lots. Terribly. Unbearably" and "I wish I could see you. . . . I'd whisper all sorts of things in your very charming ear."[4] As the days turned into weeks, the ardor of his letters increased and included schemes for Peggy to visit him.

> It wouldn't cost more than fifteen dollars at most for you to come up and it would be worth many times that to me to see you and deliver some kisses on your lips. You could borrow an overnight bag from someone at Dinglewood and put your nightie and—indelicate suggestion—in it and trot right up.[5]

After Christmas 1925 Tom and Peggy were reunited and the letters stopped. Given Boyd's philandering it is easy to suspect that the passion in his letters was the product of sexual desire alone. But, despite his past and future affairs, Tom's love for Peggy was real. He never dealt well with any prolonged separation from her and often looked to other women for comfort.

Boyd's work for the *Atlanta Georgian* served several purposes, the most important of which was the income stability that had been missing since the Boyds' trip to France. The weekly check gave them the opportunity to save the proceeds from their other writing, which would, by the end of their stay in Georgia, give them a considerable nest egg with which they would embark on the next phase of their lives. Psychologically, the newspaper work reassured Boyd that his writing was good and provided him with experiences that he could mold into novels and stories.

As a reporter Boyd had numerous duties including rewrite work, coverage of meetings and conventions, reporting from crime scenes, movie reviews, and human-interest stories. Of his first day of work he wrote Peggy:

> I had some simple stories to rewrite—then sat around—then got a story from the office—advertising scheme—did that—sat around—went to lunch after one—came back—sat around—rewrote two squibs—was told to cover a radio exposition fostered by the Journal—off for the day at three o'clock. Pretty soft.[6]

Not all of his days were so easy. About another day he wrote:

> I rushed my head off today. First I had to write a story about the Community Chest—and I had to go out and get it—I had no sooner got in and got it finished then Ball [his editor] told me to go out to Decatur with the photographer and get up a feature story about another jail delivery that took place out there. "And when you get back you might go out and see Corra Harris, she's in town. . . ." Well, I got back at half past four, having had to wait for the damned grand jury to bring in the recommendation for a new trial. It was raining and all I'd eaten were two hot dogs.[7]

Eventually, Boyd would be asked to write a series of stories on Atlanta history, and he began to push for a book review column. Despite the harried life of a reporter, he saw no reason why he should not remain in Georgia and keep his job as a newspaper man.[8]

His newspaper work left Boyd with little time to devote to creative projects. He made it clear to Perkins that he had no plans for a new novel and he did not, in fact, begin work on one until he left Georgia.[9] He did continue to write short stories. One, "The Final Word," was rejected by *Scribner's* magazine because it was too short.[10] Two others—"Indian Summer," which *Scribner's* published in its British edition, and a story about the war that appeared in *American Legion Monthly*—did sell. While in Atlanta, Boyd learned that a long story called "The Salt of the Earth" had been accepted for publication in *Scribner's* American edition the following year. The story was a true departure for Boyd. Set in Oregon and California, places Boyd had never visited, and with a plot centered on the activities of workers in a lumber camp, "The Salt of the Earth" was one of his first attempts to write about a subject with which he was not intimately familiar. When it appeared, the story brought at least two letters pointing out factual errors. Boyd's reaction to these letters was far different from the response he sent to Bridges regarding criticism of a story he wrote about the war:

> I believe an apology is due Scribner's readers by me on account of the way I mistreated distances, lumber camps and nearly everything

> else touched upon in my story, "The Salt of the Earth"; and said apology I hereby tender to (1) all people who read the story and realized that I had never been to the Northwest; (2) all people who read the story and were taken in by my glib reference to a twelve hour trip from San Francisco to Seattle, a San Francisco Station, etc, (3) Gustavus S. Paine 35 East Ninth Street, New York, New York, for annoying his sense of accuracy, and (4) Mr. J.B. Fitzgerald of Seattle for a maligning the chefs of the Northwest lumber country. Also my thanks to Mr. Paine and Mr. Fitzgerald for telling me a number of things I didn't know.[11]

Though certainly written with his tongue in his cheek, the apology clearly indicates his discomfort at having written about something that he knew little about. Throughout his career Boyd had stuck to writing about what he knew, either firsthand or through research, and the reader response to "The Salt of the Earth" seemed to confirm his unexpressed belief that he could write only from experience. He never again put his name on a piece of writing that was not a product of his actual knowledge.

Ironically, though his work as a reporter limited his output as a writer of fiction, it also provided him with the material for one of the best short stories he ever wrote. Titled "Bloodhounds," the story describes with great sympathy the capture of an African American escapee from a chain gang. Though not published until 1930 when it appeared in the *Atlantic*, the story clearly points to Boyd's opinions on race. While Boyd was not above racial stereotyping, his stay in the South opened his eyes to the injustices of a social system based on the subjugation of one race to the economic advantage of another. He enunciated his feelings about Southern society in a letter to Perkins referring to Atlanta as a "Klan ridden town" and more fully in an article published in the *Forum* titled "Defying the Klan."[12]

Only months after they settled at 26 Kirkwood Road in Atlanta, the Boyds were once again on the move. This time they landed in Chicago to visit Peggy's parents, but they planned to move on to Vermont after a brief stay. Freed from the responsibilities of newspaper work, Boyd began to think seriously about his next book. He and Peggy had begun work on a novel about the South before leaving Atlanta. They planned to finish it in Chicago and attempt to have it serialized before turning it over to a publisher. The story was the slightly fictionalized account of the events of sculptor Gutzon Borglum's life in Atlanta while working on the Confederate memorial on Stone Mountain and was intended as a light story of disappointed love.[13]

The events of everyday life interfered with the Boyds' writing and their plans to move to New England. A few days into their stay in Chicago's Plaza Hotel, Betty Grace came down with the measles, forcing them to extend their visit. When she recovered, Tom and Peggy decided to forgo the move to New England in order to extend Peggy's time with her parents before leaving Betty Grace with them and going abroad again in the fall. They took a house at 1544 East Fifty-seventh Street, but events again conspired to change their plans. That summer Peggy received an assignment from the *American Legion Monthly* in Asheville, North Carolina, leaving Tom in the unusual position of primary caregiver to his daughter.[14] The novel about the South remained incomplete.

When Peggy finished her assignment, the Boyds began making plans to move to Connecticut. They gave up their plans for another trip to Europe and instead began looking for a house in Connecticut:

> We're both bothered by roaming around and have seen enough of the country to last for awhile. . . .
>
> We are thinking of driving east of New Haven along the sea towards Stonington and Lyme and find a house to buy in that neighborhood if it is not too expensive. A farmhouse or a house on the fringe of a small town, of about nine rooms is what we are after. Our object is to get beyond commuting distance of New York as we think there will be less demand for houses that far away and that consequently there are more of them to be had.[15]

They found what they were looking for in Ridgefield, Connecticut, and moved quickly to close the sale despite the house's significant deficiencies.

In a letter to F. Scott Fitzgerald, Max Perkins expressed bemused irritation with the Boyd's snap decision-making and careless attitude:

> Tom and Peggy Boyd turned up in September in Ridgefield, Conn., about twelve miles from New Canaan. When I came back from a week's vacation they were settled there more or less, in a rented house but the house has no furnace and it gets mighty cold in Connecticut. Last week when no furnace had been installed, though long before promised, the real estate man said they were entitled to cancel the lease, and that he would help them get a house that did have a furnace; but on the way they looked at a rather fine old house which was for sale, and Tom bought it.—It has no furnace! But they don't seem to worry much.[16]

The house, only the second that Tom and Peggy had ever owned, sat behind a wrought iron fence on a large lot near the outskirts of Ridgefield. A large covered porch wrapped around much of the first story and large windows looked out on the wide lawn from the second story and finished attic. Over the next few years, Boyd would devote a great deal of time and money to making the house more comfortable and livable. Like most homes, it would be the scene of great happiness and suffering. Settled at last, Boyd again began thinking about his next book. He needed money to pay for his new home, and he was acutely aware of the necessity of producing another successful novel after the disappointment of *Samuel Drummond*.

Fortunately, Max Perkins devised a plan to do both. The market for books about the war had changed dramatically since the publication of *Through the Wheat* in 1923. Several authors had scored big financial success with novels and movie scripts dealing with the war. Fitzgerald expressed his dismay at Boyd's unfortunate timing in a 1926 letter to Perkins:

> . . . God, what bad luck Tom Boyd had! Stallings made the killing with the play and movie; Now Thomason makes a contract with

> Hearst, for a lot, I guess and Tom who came first came too early I suppose. Yet "What Price Glory?" would never have been written, I suppose, except for "Through the Wheat." Not that Tom's novel wasn't a success in a way but to make about $6,000 as an originator and see others rake it in like croupiers later—I know how bitter it must make him.[17]

Perkins was already working on a plan to allow Boyd to take advantage of the surge in interest for books about the war. By November 1926, he had developed a plan to reissue *Through the Wheat* in a special edition, adding sixteen full-page illustrations and selling it for three dollars and fifty cents.[18] Optimistic about the future sales of the new edition and in need of ready cash, Boyd asked for and received a five-hundred-dollar advance.[19]

With the advance from the new edition, the money Peggy made writing for newspaper syndicates and magazines, small payments he received for stories published in *Short Story Magazine*, and the occasional sale of a story to *Scribner's*, both Tom and Peggy were able to devote the last few months of 1926 and much of 1927 to writing novels.

Peggy completed the manuscript she had been working on for more than a year and sent it to Max Perkins in March 1927. Perkins was very disappointed in the novel. His suggestions for improvement, which amounted to an almost complete rewrite, included a shift in perspective and the excision of entire chapters.[20] Despite the size of the job, Peggy undertook and completed the revision of the manuscript within the year. Scribner's published *The Unpaid Piper* in 1927.[21]

Boyd also completed and mailed a manuscript to Max Perkins in the first months of 1927. Titled "The Wrong Diana," the manuscript arrived on Perkins's desk in May 1927 and provoked a response similar to that of Peggy's latest work. Perkins wrote a long letter in which he expressed doubts about the book, the impact it would have on Boyd's reputation as an author, and sales potential: "I must tell you that I do feel as though the book were not a success, and although its publication seems practicable, I think it should be better if you should not publish it."[22] After explaining his reservations about the book and his reasons for believing that the book would not sell, Perkins concluded:

> I think you are at a critical stage now, and that the next book ought to convince people. Your powers ought to be brought to convincing expression. They would be with a subject that was in itself impressive, because you make the most of a subject. I wish it were practicable for you therefore to try to find a large scheme for a novel that was in itself impressive, and which would attract initial attention. Then your qualities would make themselves felt.[23]

Perkins felt that Boyd was on the verge of a critical and popular breakthrough, but he was convinced that publication of "The Wrong Diana" would be a step in the wrong direction.

If Perkins hoped Boyd would take his criticism as a clear indication that "The Wrong Diana" should not be published, the reply he received must have been a disappointment. Though polite and even deferential in his reply, Boyd made it clear that he felt the book worthy of publication:

> I've thought a long while about your advice as to publication of that book and I know you spoke for my own good as much as for any other reason. Nevertheless, I feel the book ought to be published. . . . The only trouble is I shouldn't like to ask you to recommend it if you felt it was to be a failure—much as I'd prefer Scribner's to publish it. And I also realize that you have some hope that some day I may write a better book than any I've done so far and for that reason you'd not like me to change. So supposing . . . we put it this way: If you do not like the book sufficiently to recommend it with a clear conscience I will offer it elsewhere; and then if another firm takes it it will make no difference with my future books so long as you are interested to see them.[24]

Not quite an ultimatum, Boyd's letter made it clear that he intended to pursue publication of "The Wrong Diana" with or without Perkins's approval. He was no longer as willing to follow Perkins's advice about his manuscripts. Though this defiance did not immediately lead to conflict, it foreshadowed the split that Boyd would eventually make with Perkins and Scribner's. Perkins avoided a permanent rift by quickly reassuring him that he was willing to recommend publication of "The Wrong Diana" and was issuing a contract for it immediately.[25] Perkins's decision to go ahead with publication indicates his belief in Boyd's potential as an author. Though Boyd had never published a blockbuster or even produced a book that sold decently since *Through the Wheat*, Perkins was unwilling to lose him to another publisher.

Boyd's threat may have been the result of the attention being paid to him by another publishing house. As early as March 1927, Earle Balch of Minton Balch publishing company had approached Boyd with an offer for an advance on any book he chose to write.[26] By the winter of 1927, Boyd, driven by a need for quick cash, agreed to write a biography of Simon Girty, one of the most notorious renegades of colonial-era Ohio, for Minton Balch. A short time after signing the contract with Balch and receiving the five-hundred-dollar advance, a remorseful and anxious Boyd wrote Perkins to tell him.

> Now I come to a paragraph of lamentations. The night I telephoned you from Ridgefield, I wrote Earle Balch (being very much in need of money) and told him that if he still wanted to advance me five hundred dollars for the Girty book I would accept it. . . . I felt squeamish about it at the time, and more so now. But he immediately sent on the contract and the check, and while I have not cashed the check . . . I did sign the contract and I'd feel a fool for sure if I backed out again. So I suppose, unless you're interested enough to suggest some miracle, I've got to do it for them.[27]

Perkins's response was magnanimous. He told Boyd not to worry about writing for another publisher, that his relationship with Scribner's had not been damaged, and to do the best book he could for Minton Balch.[28]

Boyd produced an interesting, if flawed, biography in *Simon Girty: The White Savage*. In the biography Boyd attempted to rehabilitate the reputation of Simon Girty, who was one of the most notorious and vilified renegades on the Ohio frontier during the Revolutionary War. Clearly sympathetic toward Girty, Boyd retells the most damning events of Girty's life, such as his presence at the burning of an American officer by Native Americans, using sources that suggested that Girty consistently tried to prevent such atrocities and to save the lives of American settlers and soldiers rather than acting as an enthusiastic participant in these events. The most striking feature of the book is its compassionate portrayal of the plight of the Native Americans:

> Fairness and level-headedness are qualities not often found in accounts of that long drawn out fight for supremacy in the country northwest of the Ohio. Western historians have generally taken for granted that all of the land in North America belonged to the offspring of the Thirteen Colonies and that any attempt by the Indians to drive back the settlers was cruel, treacherous and extraordinarily criminal. . . .
>
> Why the Indian fought to keep his land in the Ohio country is obvious: it contained everything that he needed; and once driven from it there was little place else for him to go.[29]

Boyd offered a fresh perspective on Girty and Native Americans, but the biography was too thinly researched and too uncritical of its sources. Perkins may have seen the manuscript of *Simon Girty* before it was published but if he did, he expressed no interest in publishing it. He was still waiting for Boyd to produce a book he could fully support. He would not have to wait much longer.

Sometime after receiving the contract for "The Wrong Diana" in August, Boyd stopped working on that novel and began work on a new novel tentatively titled "White Man's Saga." Based on the material he had gathered for the Simon Girty book, the proposed novel told the story of a white man raised by Indians whose loyalties were torn between the Native America, British, and American interests in the years between 1774 and 1794.

Boyd's letter of introduction for the new novel brimmed with confidence. He asked about an advance for the book once it was further along and inquired about the possibility of serialization.[30] Obviously enthusiastic about the new project, Boyd worked quickly and sent the completed manuscript to Perkins on October 14. After an initial scan of the book, Perkins wrote to tell Boyd that he thought the work was good.[31] A week later he wrote to tell him that he still had not had a chance to give the book a thorough reading.[32] Lacking a definitive answer from Perkins, Boyd lost confidence in the new manuscript:

> [M]y apologies for submitting so unfinished a piece of work. But you see as usual I've been in a kind of futile tizzy. I wanted to write a good book that could come out before "The Wrong Diana"; I tried to write one perhaps I should have succeeded if I had had more time, but now I've got to do something else in order to earn or get money. . . . But when you can get at it I'd like to have your opinion of the book.[33]

On October 28, Perkins responded with a long letter in which he praised and critiqued the manuscript. He complimented Boyd for his treatment of the Native Americans, the book's authenticity, and the creation of sympathetic and interesting characters but suggested, among other things, that the historical material be reduced and that more time should be spent explaining the characters and giving clues to their emotions and interior lives.[34] Boyd set to work on the revision of the manuscript in an attempt to have it ready for spring publication.[35] By the end of November he had completed his work and resubmitted the manuscript. On December 1, Perkins wired Boyd to let him know that the novel had arrived and was, in his opinion, greatly improved. He also let Boyd know that he could arrange for a five-hundred-dollar advance.[36]

The Boyds were once again in need of money. They had relocated to the Chicago area so that Peggy could be near her mother, who had suffered a stroke.[37] They spent most of their visit living in the home of Peggy's parents, under conditions that hampered Boyd's attempts at writing. One of his first decisions regarding the new novel was to change the name from "White Man's Saga" to "Son of Long Knives," though eventually the book would become *Shadow of the Long Knives*.[38] It was during this time that Boyd began serious work on the text of the Girty biography that would be published later that year. While doing research for that book, he had come across many stories of people held captive by Native Americans during the colonial period. As a money-making scheme, he now proposed editing a collection of these stories for Scribner's. Perkins rejected the idea based on past experiences with similar books, but he did not completely close the door to proposals on similar subjects.[39] At the end of January 1928, Boyd wrote Perkins to ask for the remaining two hundred dollars from his advance, and to inform Perkins that he would be staying at The Harvard Club in Chicago. His stated reason for moving out of his in-laws' house was that he could not work in the crowded conditions, but there was another reason for his move that he would divulge to Perkins only later.[40]

The Boyds' marriage was in trouble again. While living in Chicago, Tom revealed or Peggy discovered that he had been having an affair. The affair had taken place during the fall and winter of 1927. The Boyds had moved to an inn in New Canaan to avoid the cold when the radiator they had installed in their home failed and the water pipes froze. While Peggy was in Boston working for a newspaper syndicate, Tom had entered into a relationship with an older woman named Louise.[41] Those familiar with the people living in New Canaan at the time of the affair might be tempted, due to the circumstantial evidence, to assume that the Louise was Louise Perkins, wife of his editor Max Perkins. While the Perkinses' marriage was occasionally tense, there is no evidence to suggest that Louise Perkins was unfaithful to her husband with Thomas Boyd or anybody else.[42]

Near the end of February, Peggy drove back to Ridgefield with Betty Grace, leaving Tom in Chicago.[43] On the way home, a truck that Peggy was attempting to pass forced her off the road and into a ditch.[44] Though Tom rarely wrote Perkins concerning his personal life, he did include one passage that should have signaled to Perkins the serious nature of the break between Tom and Peggy:

> If you are ever about Ridgefield I wish you'd call or stop and see her. She doesn't like most people generally but she thinks you're one of the nicest and decentest (which I'm most certainly not) person in the world.[45]

Things had deteriorated rapidly while the Boyds were in Chicago, and in the weeks following Peggy's return to Ridgefield they contemplated a divorce.

The letters written by Tom and Peggy during this period of separation provide rare insight into the depth of their feelings for one another. In a letter written shortly after Peggy left for Ridgefield, as a response to a letter Peggy had written to him, Tom attempted to explain his actions and his feelings about the future of their marriage:

> I don't know what else to say. Your letter of Monday was very nice but I don't feel either tender or true. I am still upset. . . . As I've told you a million times I was never in love with Louise. I cannot say as much about Sandra. I've told you that too. However, I'm sure nothing definite will come of it. That is all I can tell you. Except that I've met nobody here that I'm in love with.
>
> You see I'm trying to explain my situation—I'm very fond of you and of Betty Grace. You are very nice to tell me you are willing for me to come back. But for me it is not so easy. I don't want to come back with the feeling I've nowhere else to go—I don't want to be pulled or driven back. As I said before I want to be free.
>
> And I want you to feel like that. You are young and attractive and there may be much more in life than I can give you. I am sure you have felt that. So do what you like and I will respect the same convention you have decided on toward me.[46]

The letter makes Boyd's feelings plain. While he still felt love for Peggy, he did not want to be romantically restrained by their marriage. In a reversal of the depth of feeling evident in the early days of their relationship, Peggy's reply clearly indicated that she was willing to agree to a continuation of their marriage under any circumstance:

> I certainly think that you are quite right about feeling that you don't want to come back with the feeling that you are doing it because you have nowhere else to go. Neither do I want you quite under those circumstances. I am trying not to drive or pull you back. I am sure you see very clearly about it—more so than I perhaps. You too are young, and you should spend your life with someone you love, and someone who loves you. I will say this much however: I love you so much that it does not matter to me *what* you do—in any way. Behave as you please. I know what you are—unselfish, struggling always to do the right thing—and I know it from years of experience with you. You have made mistakes, yes, but you have never done wrong. You are fully capable of judging for yourself what you want. *But* if such a dire calamity as you suggest should happen: if it should become true that you literally have no place to go—you must feel that you can always come home. If the grocery bill remains unpaid, and the coal man threatens in the offing, no matter what, I will keep enough money in the bank for you to come home on, if you need to come. In sickness or trouble you must come to me.[47]

Boyd lived with friend John Becker in Chicago for another month and continued work on the biography of Simon Girty and the proofs of *Shadow of the Long Knives*. But by the end of March he had returned to Ridgefield and domestic concerns involving faulty furnaces and house painting.[48]

Despite the marital turmoil of the early months of the year, 1928 was one of the most prosperous years of Tom and Peggy's life together. By the time of his return to Ridgefield, Boyd had earned $1,200. He had successfully placed stories in *Scribner's*, and the new illustrated edition of *Through the Wheat*, which had been published in the fall of 1927, had sold almost one thousand copies by February 1928.[49] In addition, he had received a five-hundred-dollar advance for *Shadow of the Long Knives*. For once the Boyds were on firm financial footing. The real financial windfall would come with the publication of *Shadow of the Long Knives* in May 1928 during what Max Perkins described as "a terrible spring" for book sales.[50]

Shadow of the Long Knives tells the story of Angus McDermott, a white man who had been raised by Native Americans along the Ohio frontier in the years leading up to the American Revolution. McDermott had worked for the British during their attempts to quell the Native American insurrections in the 1760s, and his loyalty to the British and Native Americans who had raised him put McDermott on the wrong side of both the Revolutionary War and the Battle of Fallen Timbers. The battles are described in great detail and the Native Americans portrayed with great sympathy. As he had in his biography of Simon Girty, Boyd provided his readers with the unique perspective of the Native Americans on important historic events. His description of the British refusal to help the Native Americans after the Battle of Fallen Timbers is typical:

> The British were there to help: they had promised the Indians support not only in keeping the ground on which they now lived but also in winning back all of the country west and north of the Ohio from the settlers. And yet at this crucial time the guns were silent and the bayonets were sharply pointed against the breasts of those who had fled there for security! McDermott's mind could not take it in. . . . But he felt the treachery in his heart, as strongly as if it had been directed against himself.[51]

Despite an awkwardly rendered romance between McDermott and his wife, the relationship with his son who opposes his father's choice of allies rings true. The novel drew on Boyd's strengths as a writer: his ability to describe the heat, smell, and feel of battle and his familiarity with Ohio and its history. As such, it was one of his best books and led to a new and prosperous phase of his career.

The book was well received by critics, though it drew less attention than his earlier works. The *New York Times* announced, "Here is another good story by the man who wrote "Through the Wheat." . . . the thoroughness with which Mr. Boyd seems to have absorbed his material and the superb simplicity of his style make this a novel that should be widely read."[52] A review that appeared in the Sunday magazine section of the *Providence Journal* concurred:

> This is a novel about Indians, Indian-fighting, frontier scouts, continental troops and British redcoats. Let me say in the very first paragraph that I was enormously taken with it, that I read it with inordinate relish, that I commend it whole-heartedly to all orders of readers, whether critics or sheer good story hunters.[53]

While the reviews must have pleased both Boyd and Perkins, the sales of the book brought both men greater satisfaction.

Between *Through the Wheat* in 1923 and *Shadow of the Long Knives* in 1928, Scribner's accepted and published three books by Thomas Boyd that had collectively sold fewer than nine thousand copies. The low sales must have shaken Perkins's faith in Boyd's future as a publishing author, but *Shadow of the Long Knives* changed that. Less than one month after publication, the novel had sold 2,480 copies, covering the advance and prompting Perkins to write, "You are truly most excellently fitted for novels that deal with the past. There is no doubt about it. You seem to have the rare genius of the past and the power to recreate it."[54] By June 14 the book had sold an additional 710 copies and would clear sales of 5,823 copies by the end of November, earning Tom more than two thousand dollars in royalties in 1928.[55]

The money earned by *Shadow of the Long Knives* allowed Boyd to make improvements to the Ridgefield house and the opportunity to concentrate on his next writing project. Perkins had expressed concern about the effects of the distractions of Boyd's personal life on his work in a letter written just after the publication of *Shadow of the Long Knives*:

> It seems to me truly marvelous that you have produced as much as you have done under the conditions that have surrounded you. If

> you ever had a full year in which to write a book, without any kind of interruption except the little ones that nobody can avoid, the qualities that you had would make it something that would go far. Not only that, but they truly are qualities which make for popularity. They are not the light and flashy qualities such as characterize the hits of the month or so. They are qualities of sympathetic understanding, and of deep feeling, and a sense of the fundamental things. I think when you get the idea for a book that you generally rush at it and crowd it to a finish, and that would be alright if you belonged to the first class of writers I mention, perhaps. But the sort of novel you write requires quite a lot of reflection. . . . I feel like a school teacher, and so will stop.[56]

As a rule, Perkins's advice to Tom about his work was less direct. Tom's response indicated that Perkins's letter caught him somewhat off guard, but that he agreed with Perkins's assessment:

> I've wanted to write ever since I got your letter . . . but I haven't known just what to say. . . . I must tell you I didn't think it preaching at all: you're quite right, I've rushed into everything I've ever done, but in the case of my books the circumstances have been almost unavoidable, for I've never had enough money to carry me through to the end of one of them while I was writing. But it is my intention from now on to take more time and care even if I have to stop in the middle and take it up again months later.[57]

Boyd took Perkins's advice seriously and the money from his last book gave him a chance to fulfill his plans for writing his next.

Boyd's biography of Simon Girty was also published in 1928. And, though he was disappointed in the result, Boyd decided that his next book would be another biography. For his subject he again returned to his Ohio roots by selecting the founder of Defiance and the hero of the Battle of Fallen Timbers, General Anthony Wayne. On June 26, Boyd wrote to Perkins to propose the idea, "[N]ext to Arnold he was the most gallant officer in the revolution."[58] Perkins's reply was overwhelmingly positive: "We require no time to tell you that we are emphatically for the life of Anthony Wayne. . . . I believe it is a very good plan and will turn out to be at least a satisfactory and remunerative one from your point of view."[59] Perkins would once again prove to be a good predictor of the book market and an astute judge of his author's strengths and weaknesses.

Buoyed by Perkins's enthusiasm for the Wayne biography, Boyd began work on the book ahead of schedule. Though he had not planned on starting until the fall of 1928, on August 6 he wrote Perkins to ask for an advance and to inform him of his progress. According to Boyd, he had completed 40,000 words and believed he would be able to complete the book by the new year.[60] Perkins wired him one thousand dollars against all future earnings and encouraged Boyd to send any completed portions to *Scribner's* magazine to help them make selections for publication.[61] Boyd's reply indicated his intent to dedicate himself to the writing of the Wayne biography:

> I wrote to tell you that I had begun the Wayne biography and that I hoped to be finished by Christmas. That was a mistake. I doubt that I'll be finished before spring. Not that it isn't going well enough; it is. But I want first to write out all the material I have just as if I were making a final draft, then go down to Washington and Philadelphia where I will get much more material; and then I want to write it all over as if it were a new book.[62]

Confidence in Boyd at Scribner's was high. On the strength of the success of *Shadow of the Long Knives*, Perkins was able to offer him a two-thousand-dollar advance and 15 percent royalties on copies of the Wayne biography.[63]

Boyd stuck to his plans for researching the biography, if not his timetable. In mid-September he sent a rough version of the completed manuscript to Perkins and Robert Bridges, *Scribner's* magazine editor, for an initial reaction.[64] Having begun his research at the library at Columbia University, he traveled in October 1928 to Philadelphia, where the local historical society gave him access to mountains of information.[65] The first four chapters of the book were completed by November 6, and the entire manuscript was mailed to Perkins and Robert Bridges on December 1.[66] The manuscript impressed Bridges, who agreed to publish five chapters of the biography at a rate of $250 apiece. The five segments would detail Wayne's early life, his experiences at Valley Forge and Monmouth, his victory at Stony Point, his role in the siege of Yorktown, and a description of the Northwest Campaign against the Indians.[67]

By the time Boyd received the second thousand dollars from his advance, the Wayne biography had earned him a total of $3,250 on a book that had not yet been published. Perkins seemed confident in Boyd's ability and future.

> Anyhow, I suppose you realize that your position as a writer is a strong one which commands the respect of the critics, including those whose opinion has weight and value. This cannot be said of many writers. There are few who have not written something specious and trivial. The Mad Anthony is certainly a very fine piece of work, and all your work gives one a feeling of growth and increasing power.[68]

The kind words from Perkins and the eagerness of *Scribner's* magazine for chapters of *Mad Anthony Wayne* for publication boosted Boyd's confidence in his abilities and turned his plans for future writing to biography and history. In late January he wrote Perkins explaining his newfound interest in history and offering a fair assessment of his talent:

> I like to read into things and inform myself. I'm better at explaining than inventing, which would point to the suggestion that, when I've the proper equipment, I might do better at biography than at fiction. If I felt positive that the Mad Anthony was a really valuable book, I think I'd begin to write another.[69]

He would have to wait until August for critical or fiscal proof of the value of his biography. Perkins held publication of the entire book until the five excerpts had appeared in the March through July issues of *Scribner's*, and, as was typical of Boyd's life, many things would change in the intervening months.

The year 1929 certainly seemed a promising one for Tom and Peggy. Tom spent most of the first eight months of the year communicating with Perkins and Bridges about aspects of publishing *Mad Anthony Wayne*, engaging in extensive and expensive home repairs, and writing and thinking about writing.

He and Peggy had embarked on a series of writing projects together that proved fairly lucrative. Working together, they wrote formula novels for serialization in the *Popular Magazine*.[70] One of these novels earned the Boyds nine hundred dollars.[71] Boyd was never completely comfortable with the pulp novels he wrote with his wife, but he continued to do them because of the money. Thomas Boyd, unlike other more notable authors, never forgot that writing was a job and that the point of any job was to earn money to make a living. Consequently, he took work when and where he could find it. When he and Peggy needed money to buy the Ridgefield house, he had agreed to ghostwrite *Mostly Mississippi*, a posthumous book by Herbert Quick, for Henry Holt. Later he rewrote a book by Willoughby Sharpe, *The Murder of an Honest Broker*.[72] As the Boyds' earnings from 1928 dwindled, Boyd continued not only to work on serializations, but also to write and sell several of what he called "cheap stories" to make ends meet.[73]

It is a testament to the Boyds' lack of fiscal responsibility that despite the money they earned in 1928 and 1929 as well as the income from *Mad Anthony Wayne*, they could end up once again in desperate need of money.[74] According to the Boyds' 1928 tax return, they earned $5,624 dollars, a little more than one hundred dollars a week and more than enough to support a family of three and establish some savings.[75] But the Boyds were incapable of managing their money well. Their bank statement of May 1929 illustrates their lack of fiscal sense. On April 30 they had a balance of $408.70; by May 31 they had a balance of $72.59; and as Boyd's own figuring on the statement shows, they had spent all but $28.51 by the time the statement arrived.[76] The source of their expenses in 1929 was home repairs. With time on his hands awaiting publication of the Wayne biography, Boyd embarked on a massive remodeling project at the Ridgefield house. He paid off the furnace, painted the house, had five large windows custom made, had the front of the house lowered and a new roof put on, converted two rooms into one, and repaired the fireplace.[77] The end result of all the repairs and spending was that by the middle of June he was writing to Max Perkins to tell him of his imminent financial collapse:

> I can only say that I've managed things rather poorly from a financial point and that I'll be a pauper so far as available funds go by the first of June. When I wrote you last summer about the life of Wayne I had in mind that there would be a surplus from the advance with which I could write something else. But whatever surplus there was, plus a couple of thousand dollars, went into this confounded house.[78]

Fortunately, help would soon arrive in the form of an advance for a new book that Boyd had proposed to Perkins the month before.

On April 16, Boyd had written Perkins to tell him that although he had not begun another book, he was thinking of writing another biography and was considering Alexander Hamilton for the subject of that book.[79] Perkins, confident in the quality of the Wayne biography, reassured him that he and Scribner's would welcome another biography but warned of the difficulty of a subject as multifaceted and complex as Hamilton.[80] A week later, doubting his ability to thoroughly research a comprehensive biography of Hamilton, Boyd wrote Perkins and suggested a biography of the British Revolutionary War general Cornwallis as an alternative.[81] Perkins again encouraged him to pursue his interests, but pointed out the difficulties inherent in such a book.[82] Boyd then returned to Hamilton, this time proposing to write only about Hamilton's personal life.[83] But doubts remained and before the end of April, Boyd wrote again, suggesting the possibilities of a biography of

Ethan Allen, Davy Crockett, Light Horse Harry Lee, or Francis Marion.[84] In the end Tom returned to Hamilton as the subject of his next book. On May 31 Perkins sent Boyd a check for one thousand dollars as advance on the Hamilton book and Scribner's issued a contract for the book on June 26, 1929.[85] Boyd's indecisiveness indicated his discomfort with his chosen subject. Throughout his career Boyd found it difficult to write about subjects to which he felt no connection, and he would eventually change the subject of the biography again to a subject with which he was more familiar and whose life and career resembled that of Anthony Wayne.

The thousand dollars was, no doubt, welcome. Boyd's books in print had earned only $116.52 between February 1 and June 29, 1929. As with his other books, in the days leading up to its publication Boyd worried about the money his Wayne biography would earn as well as its critical acceptance.[86] In July, he learned that a motion picture company was interested in purchasing the movie rights to his short story "The Long Shot," which had been included in his short story collection *Points of Honor*.[87] This event not only put money in his pocket but planted in his mind the idea that Hollywood might provide the answers to his financial difficulties.

As often seemed true of Thomas Boyd's life, just as his professional life seemed to be on track, his personal life fell apart. After returning to Peggy in Ridgefield, Boyd met and attracted the attention of another woman. Ruth Fitch Bartlett, daughter of a Milwaukee banker, Vassar graduate, wife of an unfaithful businessman, resident of New Canaan, Connecticut, and friend of Max Perkins, had fallen in love with Boyd—and he with the attention of an older woman. When Peggy learned of their affair she finally decided that she could no longer stay married to Tom. She confronted Ruth at Tom's thirty-first birthday and later had it out with Tom. He left that same night.[88] Later that summer Tom and Ruth traveled to Canada to visit his relatives, effectively ending any chance of reconciliation with Peggy.[89] In a story titled "Extreme Mental Cruelty," published in the *Ladies Home Journal* in 1930, Boyd's main character expresses feelings about the end of his marriage that may have reflected Boyd's own feelings about the end of his marriage to Peggy:

> His throat tightened as if he were to choke with sympathy for both of them. Seven years they had been married. It was an enormous chunk out of both of their youths. Though they were still under thirty, they had since the beginning gone from love and a scrimping salary, through disillusionment and readjustment, but had arrived at a companionable fondness for each other and a future comparatively free of care. And now all those years, their joys and hardships, were to have gone for nothing; lying there, he held that aching thought in his mind with stubborn wretchedness.[90]

From 1929 on, Thomas Boyd would navigate the world without the counsel of the woman who had given him a child, a sense of self-esteem, and a career. Not surprisingly, his life became more erratic than ever.

Boyd had enjoyed the economic success and stability enjoyed by the country during the 1920s. Despite poor financial decision-making, he had been able to support his family and buy a home. As the summer of 1929 came to a close, Boyd had earned money from a book that had yet to be published and from a book he could not even describe. He had every reason to be optimistic about the future, but just as the economic course of the country was changed by the stock market crash of 1929, his divorce would alter his life profoundly and not for the better.

chapter seven

"I must say I am worried about your plans for writing"

Tom and Ruth Boyd began their life together in Metis Beach, Ontario, on a visit to his father's family. They rented a cottage near the banks of the St. Lawrence River where Boyd tried to write and he and Ruth began to plan their lives together. A fit, capable, attractive, and charming woman, Ruth Fitch Bartlett Boyd was an amateur poet and writer. She was a born organizer who had for years organized her own life and would in the years to come attempt to organize Tom's.[1] The first order of business was the divorce and the second to find a place to live and a place where Boyd could start writing again. Things would not go as smoothly as Ruth hoped. Before finally settling in Vermont in 1932, they would follow Boyd's work prospects across the country and back while their relationship withered and his earning power diminished.

The new couple spent August and the first week of September in Canada before driving back to New York so that Tom could take care of some business with Scribner's.[2] By September 27, 1929, they had moved to Reno,

Nevada, in order to obtain divorces from their spouses. On November 12, Peggy received a letter from the Reno law firm of Thatcher and Woodburn informing her that Tom had hired them to handle the divorce and explaining that things would proceed much more quickly if he were listed as the plaintiff and she the defendant.[3] Though no record of Peggy's response remains, she must have gone along with the plan outlined by Tom's lawyers. The divorce was finalized shortly after Boyd met the three-month residency requirement. Although the exact terms of the divorce are not specifically spelled out in the correspondence, Tom sent checks for $150 to Peggy as child support and got to spend at least some time with Betty Grace in the summer of every year.

Over the next five years, Tom and Peggy exchanged numerous letters. Most were friendly, businesslike letters about Betty Grace and her health and education. Some were angry and some of Boyd's were apologetic, particularly when he could not send the money he owed Peggy. Often, his letters were encouraging, expressing concern for her future well-being and even offering advice. Some of the letters were scolding, but many offered her reassurances. After Peggy spent a wild weekend in New York, during which she got into some sort of trouble that Tom learned about secondhand, he wrote:

> I didn't know what to make of it except foolishness. Then your letter came and of course it disturbed me very much. I thought you were bound to wake up to your responsibilities, but apparently it will take longer than is good. You are a very fine person, but you ought to think more of what you say and do—what kind of life you want I can't imagine—perhaps you really like running about New York in that mad way, but I can't believe it—though if you do I have nothing to say except that I'll always be fond of you and glad to help you as far as I can—whatever.[4]

Another letter either related to the New York event or some other upheaval in Peggy's life was less harsh and more encouraging:

> If you can get a good grip on your life you will be doing something of inestimable value to yourself. That is the first thing you should try to do, it seems to me. Then there would be no chance of you getting socked, no matter what happens.[5]

Finally, when Peggy wrote to Tom expressing serious self-doubt about her character and future, he responded with a letter encouraging her to move on in her life and open herself up to new people:

> It was certainly worth something to get that silly idea out of your head—that you were a young, pretty pariah among mankind and received friendship from nobody. What started it I can't imagine, but I always knew you had many admirers and would have many more if you let them get close enough to see you. . . . I'll naturally always be interested in you.[6]

Peggy would meet someone new. She married Ted Shane, an editor at *Judge* magazine, in 1930. She continued to write, concentrating on movie scripts and Broadway plays, and despite the period immediately after the dissolution of her marriage to Boyd, she lived a life considerably calmer than that of her ex-husband.

Life in Reno, Nevada, was not pleasant for Boyd. Removed from his friends and research materials, he began writing short stories again to pass the time and pay the bills. According to a November letter to Perkins, Boyd had finished six stories since the end of July. Three of these were published in 1930: "The Mayor of Benburry" in the *Ladies' Home Companion*, "Extreme Mental Cruelty" in *Ladies' Home Journal*, and "Resident of Purgatory" in *Harper's*. Two of the three drew on his recent experiences. "Extreme Mental Cruelty" was an emotional story of the breakup of a marriage, and "Resident of Purgatory" described the life among the temporary, divorce-seeking community and the permanent citizens of Reno who depended on them for money. For Boyd the time in Reno began a lifestyle much different from his previous life. He did more drinking than he had ever done before, and his drinking and hatred of his situation led to a fight in a bar and a night in jail.[7]

Though he had success writing short stories while in Nevada, his time in Reno had a negative impact on his biography of Alexander Hamilton. He wrote Perkins that

> [T]here's not much that can be done with Hamilton so far away from sources—at least I'm going to live in Vermont—in South Woodstock in a brick house on a back road which is lovely—if I'm alive by the time I can leave this purgatory on earth.[8]

Following Boyd's return to the East Coast, he would live in a house just like the one he described, but he would never complete a biography of Alexander Hamilton.

Scribner's published Boyd's biography of Anthony Wayne in October 1929. *Mad Anthony Wayne* verged on hagiography. Wayne's exploits as a Revolutionary War general and as the leader of the American expedition to secure the Ohio frontier make up the majority of the biography, and in each action Boyd portrays Wayne as the hero, the man whose ideas almost always prove correct, and the leader whose decisions make the differences in battle. The battles are explained in detail, and Boyd again displayed his talent for describing warfare. Though he did extensive research, consulting both primary and secondary sources, Boyd avoided presenting the biography as a scholarly work. In his biography of Simon Girty, Boyd had attempted to rehabilitate Girty's reputation; in his biography of Anthony Wayne, Boyd tried to resuscitate the memory of a man that he felt history and the general public had unfairly slighted.

As usual, Boyd worried about the book's sales and critical reception. The reviews were good, praising the book's ability to capture a sense of action and its descriptions of battle. The review in the *Bookman* was typical:

> Because its subject was so essentially a man of action, the biography has no trouble in remaining dramatic. And because Wayne

> had little to do with social forces that led to Revolution, Mr. Boyd has wisely limited his biography to a succession of dramatic actions.[9]

The reviewer from the *New York Herald Tribune* came closest to affirming that Boyd had accomplished his goals in the Wayne biography:

> It is an unpretentious book, without the paraphernalia of scholarship, but bearing in its pages the unmistakable marks of careful study and intimacy with the scenes and characters of Wayne's life that gives it a flavor of authenticity and reality that is denied to many a more imposing tome.[10]

With the solid critical reception of the book assured, Perkins and Boyd waited for the sales returns. By November 18, the biography had sold 3,040 copies; and through the holiday season and the first week of February 1930 it sold an additional 1,700 copies.[11] The success of the Wayne biography and in particular the praise of his ability to depict scenes of action influenced Boyd's choice of subjects for his next work.

Thomas Boyd and Ruth Fitch were married in December 1929 close on the heels of their Reno divorces. They spent Christmas in Milwaukee with Ruth's family and then traveled to New York, where they stayed for two months. While there Boyd decided to write a biography of American Revolutionary War general and Wayne's contemporary Light Horse Harry Lee. This decision took him to Richmond, Virginia, to do research.[12] On February 12, 1930, he wrote Perkins from the Jefferson Hotel outlining his plans for research for the next few months. Tom and Ruth would stay in Richmond until April and then go on research jaunts to Lexington, Stratford, Fredericksburg, Alexandria, and Baltimore before returning to the Northeast.[13] As with his Wayne biography, Boyd took research on his Lee book seriously. In poring over Lee's correspondence while he was governor of Virginia and his memoirs, Boyd gained a deep respect for Lee as a man with ideas very different from what he expected:

> It may make an extraordinarily good biography, for he was a strange brilliant man and much contrast can be developed. How odd of him to be down on slavery so that his son Robert E., getting out a new edition of his father's memoirs, could sit down directly after the Civil War and read over those words which were so against the things for which he had fought.[14]

On April 7 he wrote Perkins asking for an introduction to someone at the Library of Congress, and three weeks later he had read through much of the correspondence that existed between Lee and other Revolutionary luminaries including Hamilton, Madison, Henry, and Washington.[15] By May 15, Boyd had completed his research and planned to begin writing. He predicted that his first draft would not be complete until October.[16] Hoping that he could again have the good fortune to have excerpts published, Boyd sent the first completed chapter to *Scribner's* magazine on June 10.[17] By August, he had completed his first draft, but he still struggled with technical aspects of some of the battles.[18] The completed manuscript was sent to Perkins in mid-October.[19] Perkins wrote suggesting a small change to the beginning of the book and enclosed a check for half the two thousand dollar advance Scribner's had agreed to pay Boyd for the biography.[20]

The advance money helped Boyd, who was determined not to live off his wife's money, to set his finances in order and to smooth his ruffled feathers over *Scribner's* magazine's refusal to publish any of the chapters of the Lee biography. He had a premonition that his relationship with the magazine had come to an end when he learned that editor Robert Bridges had been forced out and replaced by Alfred Dashiell:

> I understand Mr. Bridges is out of the magazine. . . . I suppose it was inevitable and necessary, but you know I can't help feeling sorry as the devil about it. I've only had about one note from Mr. Dashiell in my life and so will feel still more of a stranger to the magazine.[21]

A few days after submitting his first chapters to the magazine, Boyd received a note from Dashiell that must have confirmed his suspicions. In response he dashed off an angry letter to Perkins:

> The enclosed note puts me in a perplexing position. Since my Wayne chapters were not indifferently received I had rather counted on a similar arrangement, so far as the magazine is concerned for the Lee book.
>
> I am sorry I was mistaken. And I realize that the magazine is much better now than it was when my Wayne articles appeared in it. . . .
>
> I should have been glad of an answer to my letter written to you ten days since—heretofore you have been interested enough in what I have submitted to give me your own opinions.[22]

Perkins replied with a letter that soothed Boyd temporarily, but it also opened the door for future confusion about the placement of chapters from the Lee biography in the magazine:

> The fact that the magazine did not take that first chapter has no bearing on later ones. What they would want to do would be . . . to use certain complete episodes in Lee's life, and the subject of the one you sent was not of a character to make it a good article. . . .
>
> Would it be possible for you, without danger to the whole work, to do several scattered chapters here and there in the biography, including several with lots of action? . . . As for us, the fact that we did not take that first chapter has nothing to do with our general inclination to use several from the later ones in the biography.[23]

The last paragraph of Perkins's letter led Boyd to conclude that the magazine would take chapters from the Lee biography that included descriptions of battles and other action. He wrote Perkins to inform him that he would develop chapters for that purpose and send them when they were ready.[24]

Given Boyd's assumptions, Dashiell's response in which he indicated that he felt there had been too much battle in the magazine in recent issues must have proven a shock.[25] Boyd's next letter expressed his disappointment at the rejection and his belief that he had been misled about the magazine's willingness to take chapters:

> I'm sorry to cause so much bother over these chapters. But since war material is ruled out and the early chapters too dull I really don't see how you are going to find—or rather how I am going to find sufficient material in the manuscript . . . for the four episodes you said you would publish.[26]

Despite his disappointment and, perhaps, driven by his desire for financial independence, Boyd suggested and submitted other chapters to the magazine when he finished the biography.[27] A second letter from Alfred Dashiell ended Boyd's last hope of getting any Lee chapters in *Scribner's* magazine:

> It does not seem to me that any of the chapters can stand alone, but a piece might be written for the magazine using the Baltimore Riot as a nucleus—that is, you could summarize the brilliance of his early career and the irony of his being beaten by a rioting mob after having passed through the Revolution unscathed. In other words, what we would want would be a portrait of "Light Horse Harry Lee" emphasizing the latter part of his career and trying to get what sort of man he really was: Whether he was a brilliant man who had tough luck or a rascal.[28]

Boyd's reply to Perkins expressed his hurt feelings and a sense of being wronged by Perkins and Scribner's in general:

> I am enclosing Dashiell's letter which is a blow to all my hopes—of course I won't rewrite the book and tag it on to the Baltimore Riot chapter for two hundred and fifty dollars or perhaps less. From your

> earlier letters I had believed that the magazine would take three or four articles, which would have given me seven hundred fifty or a thousand dollars and it is very disappointing to be flatly informed otherwise.[29]

Perhaps given the large advance he had been given on the Lee biography, Boyd's attitude about the affair with *Scribner's* magazine seemed haughty. However, at the time of the rejection of the Lee chapters, Boyd was enjoying a decent success with the Wayne biography; and the Wayne chapters that appeared in the magazine had been well received. Given these factors, he had good reason to believe that he could repeat the arrangement with the Lee biography and thereby help ensure its success. Rightly or wrongly, the incident with the magazine damaged Boyd's faith in Scribner's. He would never publish again in *Scribner's* magazine, and his relationship with Max Perkins would never again be what it had been.

As soon as he completed work on the Lee biography, Boyd began pursuing other writing projects. Probably at his wife's suggestion, Boyd traveled to Annapolis, Maryland, to begin researching the life of John Fitch, the inventor of the steamboat and one of Ruth's ancestors. Near the end of November he wrote Perkins to explain that he was having Fitch's autobiography typed in order to make it publishable. Boyd probably hoped that its publication could be arranged through Scribner's. He also informed Perkins of his intention to write a novel about life in Reno and possibly a historical novel set during the Revolutionary War.[30] A few days later he wrote Perkins to test his willingness to support a biography of Fitch. To convince him of the viability of such a book, Boyd gave a brief overview of the major events of Fitch's life and a summary of the sources to which he had access.[31] Perkins expressed doubts about the sales such a book would have in the depressed market for books and instead encouraged Boyd to write another historical novel. To provide extra incentive, he offered Tom a one-thousand-dollar advance on such a book.[32] Boyd responded by asking Perkins to wait until he had seen the material to make up his mind and indicated that he might be willing to write another historical novel.[33] If this letter caused Perkins consternation, Boyd's next letter must have dismayed him. At the end of the letter written in mid-December, Boyd included a list of books that he wanted to write. That list included a biography of Fitch, a book of short biographical pieces about Revolutionary War figures like Allen McLane and William Kirkwood, and a biography of Alexander Hamilton.[34] Perkins responded by cautioning Boyd about his plans and again attempted to remind Tom of commercial considerations:

> I must say, I am worried about your plans for writing in the future. You must not do what you are not moved to do, just because it may be expedient. I understand that view and sympathize with it. At the same time I can not think that you could hope to get a pecuniary return on the two books you spoke of which would be anywhere nearly in proportion to the work that would be entailed. I have thought about those plans many times since I saw you, and with every inclination to be persuaded to your opinion, but I can not manage it. The commercial requirements in publishing have become more exacting, and the consideration of intrinsic value—such as that would come from the historical importance of what you plan—less effective. The market is so crowded with books, competition so acute, and people so much more inclined apparently, to travel in flocks even in their reading that it is harder to get an adequate sale for the sort of books you speak of. On the other hand, you have a great gift for narratives of action, and this can be displayed both in biography and history, but hardly in the type which you are considering.[35]

This letter should have been a clear signal to Boyd about his prospects for publishing books other than biographies of major figures and historical novels. Unfortunately, Boyd would ignore most of Perkins's advice, to the detriment of his career and his relationship with Scribner's. At the time, other opportunities distracted Boyd from any serious writing project.

Early in 1931, Boyd received word that R.K.O. Pictures was interested in having him prepare a script for a realistic movie about World War I. One of Boyd's former commanders, Major General Logan Feland, who was retired and living in San Francisco, had grown tired of seeing inaccurate and romantic depictions of the war in film. Feland had gone to an executive and World War I veteran at R.K.O. to suggest that the studio produce a realistic war picture and informed them that Thomas Boyd would be the man to write it.[36] Boyd received word of R.K.O.'s interest through his agent, but the matter remained unsettled for a few weeks. The delay drove him to the point of despair:

> If this Hollywood business doesn't get settled soon I'm going to drink myself into forgetfulness. So damned much could be done with the money. I get empty headed thinking about it. And every once in a while there's a great rift in the summer cloud dream and I look down into the gloomy depths of how badly off I'll be if I don't go—Fitch not half done, no money, responsibilities, debts, Yo Ho![37]

As R.K.O. weighed the possibilities of hiring Boyd to write the treatment, he found it impossible to write anything. Finally, driven by financial desperation, Boyd took matters into his own hands by writing to General Feland and telling him that he would agree to any arrangement and would only need ten weeks to complete the script.[38] His direct letter brought results. By mid-March 1931, Boyd was on board the Santa Fe Chief bound for Hollywood.

Boyd's plan was to travel to San Francisco, where he would meet with General Feland and discuss his ideas for the screenplay before moving on to Hollywood. Once there he would complete a scenario of the movie and be prepared to turn it into a full-fledged script if the R.K.O. officials approved.[39] Boyd was accompanied on the train ride by Katherine Brown, a representative of the movie company. Though at first he thought of her "as typical movie business" and was often discouraged by her comments about what would be expected of him in Hollywood, she came to be one of his closest Hollywood friends and his most trusted advisor.[40] In a letter written to Ruth after his move from San Francisco to Hollywood, Boyd described

Mrs. Brown and lamented the fact she would be returning to the East Coast before Ruth could meet her:

> If you can imagine an encient [*sic*] woman, rather dumpy even normally as to figure, who beneath her coat and orchids dresses slightly dowdily and talks hardboiled language out of the corner of her mouth—if you can imagine such a person being attractive then you've a wonderful imagination. But as a matter of fact she is.[41]

The departure of Katherine Brown from California was one of the many ominous occurrences that signaled trouble during Boyd's stay in Hollywood.

The first thing that went wrong was Boyd's meeting with General Feland. Feland had few notions about how to make a story dramatic or appealing and, according to Boyd, most of his knowledge of the war had to do with strategy and not the realities that confronted the soldiers in the field.[42] By the end of his stay in San Francisco, Boyd had come to the conclusion that General Feland was more interested in reminiscing about the war than in helping him write a movie script.[43] When he got to Hollywood and met with officials from R.K.O., he got his first taste of the way things worked in Hollywood. After explaining his ideas, Boyd was informed by Leon d'Usseau, his assigned studio mentor, that "what this picture wanted was glamour." Upon hearing this Boyd informed R.K.O. president Joseph Schnitzer, vice president William LeBaron, and d'Usseau that "[Y]ou wont get any of that if General Feland or I have anything to do with it." Despite Boyd's typically blunt statements, the rest of the meeting went well, and d'Usseau arranged a room for him at the Hotel Wilcox.[44] As he began working on the scenario he often found d'Usseau, who called for numerous meetings that Boyd felt were a waste of time, more of a hindrance than a help.[45] D'Usseau also insisted on giving him private screenings of movies, events which Boyd felt had more to do with d'Usseau's personal pleasure than in showing him anything important about screenwriting.[46]

During Boyd's first few weeks in California, Scribner's published *Light Horse Harry Lee*. Like his previous biographies, his biography of Lee had an agenda. Boyd clearly set out to right what he perceived as an historical wrong. Lee, largely discredited and even somewhat reviled for some shady business deals and his ultimate bankruptcy after the Revolutionary War, fit perfectly with Boyd's growing predisposition for championing the underdog and for speaking up for those he believed had been unfairly treated by society. In *Light Horse Harry Lee,* Boyd presents Lee as the unsung hero of the Battle of Germantown, credits him with winning a small but key victory at Paulus Hook, and describes him as General Nathaniel Greene's most important lieutenant during the critical southern phase of the Revolutionary War. Boyd argues that it was Lee's forthrightness and loyalty, which prevented him from shirking responsibility for his decisions, that ultimately led to his ruin and his reputation as a crooked businessman. Like his biography of Anthony Wayne, Boyd's *Light Horse Harry Lee* was carefully researched, though it did not include footnotes or a bibliography. The Lee biography proves that Boyd had developed into a careful and thorough historian whose vivid writing brought his research to life.

A rather poignant but typical and amusing situation occurred when Boyd's complimentary author's copies of *Light Horse Harry Lee* were late in arriving. Boyd went to a local bookstore near his hotel and asked if it had a copy of his book, expecting the store clerk to say no. When, instead, the clerk brought out a copy, Boyd did not have enough money to pay for the book. To make matters worse the hotel would not cash a check for him so he had to wait until he received his first check from R.K.O. to buy his own book.[47] The reviews of *Light Horse Harry Lee* were, on the whole, positive; but the reviewers showed no real passion for the book. The review in the *Bookman* was typical:

> The book paints a vivid picture of certain phases of the Revolutionary War, and of the years immediately following; years of meanness, vituperation, scheming, braggadocio, and complete ingratitude towards those patriots who had given their blood that the Republic might be born.[48]

Positive reviews did little to generate interest among the general public. A month after its release, *Light Horse Harry Lee* had only sold 1,500 copies and its sales were already declining. Perkins blamed the low sales figures on the Depression and assured Boyd of the book's quality and importance.[49] By October 1931, the book had still not earned enough to cover the two-thousand-dollar advance Perkins had arranged for Boyd. In fact, the book never made enough money to cover the advance.[50]

While working on his movie treatment, Boyd experienced some of the glamour of Hollywood and met some of the movie stars of the era. Some made more of an impression than others. In response to a question from Peggy about romantic approaches from Hollywood actresses, he wrote, "No, I've not been besieged yet, but I do like Mary Astor."[51] He mentioned Astor, whom he apparently met more than once, in another letter: "There are lots of nice people out here and one of them is Mary Astor."[52] Though it is clear that Boyd, at least for a while, during his marriage to Ruth continued to have affairs, there is no evidence that he and Astor were more than acquaintances.[53] A more improbable meeting occurred after a busy night out on the town when he and another screenwriter went to meet a third screenwriter.

> When we arrived we were inspected through a peephole by a stocky, swarthy man in a brown suit who turned out to be the butler. At the end of a long living room beside a victrola, two women and a man were gathered. On the other side of the hall three men were drinking takela [*sic*] (a Mexican drink that I cant spell properly). One was forced on us. I downed mine with salt and then moved into the hall away from the bar. The sight and sound of the victrola was very raucous. A young, terribly made up hairless Mexican was singing and making sinuous passes with her legs and stomach. A woman in a green dress was talking loudly. The man had his back to me. Well, to make it short, I found out that the female with the writhing muscles was Lupe Velez, supposed to be a great screen star, that the woman in the green dress was Elsie Javis and that

> the tallest of the men at the bar was Gary Cooper. The Velez is his mistress.[54]

Though Boyd undoubtedly met other stars, his letters rarely contained news of the meetings or the names of the stars he met.

Most of the people Boyd became friends with in Hollywood were screenwriters. He met and spent time with the likes of Robert Benchley, Bart Cormack, and Paul Ganglin and even became reacquainted with F. Scott Fitzgerald. But his most frequent companions were Francis Farragoh and John Howard Lawson.

Francis Farragoh was a playwright turned screenwriter with leftward political leanings. He had established the New Playwrights Theatre in 1927. Boyd frequently spent time at the Farragohs' home, particularly while Ruth was still living on the East Coast. During the time that Boyd knew him, Farragoh had been loaned by Universal to work, unsuccessfully, on a picture for Gloria Swanson and United Artists.[55] Though Boyd and Farragoh remained good friends, it was John Howard Lawson who made the most important impression on him. In an early letter to Ruth shortly after meeting him for the first time, Boyd described Lawson as one of the few "completely natural people I've met here."[56] For much of his time in Hollywood, he maintained a close friendship with Lawson, going out with him at night and spending time in his office during the day. This friendship may have had an influence on Boyd's future politics. Lawson had serious left-wing political ideas, and, no doubt, he and Boyd talked about politics. In 1933, Lawson founded the Screenwriters Guild along with Lester Cole and Samuel Orvitz. Lawson joined the Communist Party in 1934.

In preparation for Ruth's arrival, Boyd had taken an apartment at 345 N. Hayworth Avenue and moved out of the Hotel Wilcox. He described the apartment to Ruth in a somewhat anxious letter:

> [I]t is quite nice. It has a bedroom with a double bed, good sized living room, dinette . . . a bath or two, plenty of closets and kitchenette all for one hundred and thirty a month. . . . I do hope you will like it. I know you can stand it for a month or two.[57]

Apparently Ruth could not stand it for very long. Shortly after she arrived in Hollywood, they moved to a house at 1881 Laurel Canyon Road. Boyd included the following description of the new house in a letter to Peggy:

> We have rented a house for the summer . . . which is at the mouth of a canyon, rather high on a hill, without other houses around it. There is a swimming pool and a nice walled in yard. There are three bedrooms and a sleeping porch.[58]

The Boyds remained in the house throughout most of their stay in California and entertained Betty Grace and Ruth's children there during the summer of 1931; eventually they were forced to move to a less expensive home in Venice, California.[59]

Unfortunately for Boyd, Hollywood would not provide the financial windfall for which he had hoped. Though his work in the movies did allow him to support his new wife and family for a little while, he ultimately failed to make a permanent place for himself as a screenwriter.

Things began well enough. After his initial meeting with the people at R.K.O., he felt confident that his script would be accepted and the movie made.[60] In his normal quick working manner Boyd completed the first draft of his script and a synopsis by the end of April 1931.[61] By the end of May he still had no definite word about the movie and had begun to doubt that he would hear anything any time soon.[62] His relationship with R.K.O. deteriorated over the summer of 1931, and by August he understood that the screenplay had been rejected.[63] Not surprisingly, Boyd felt that he had been badly treated. Over the summer R.K.O. had sent him conflicting signals about the movie's future, first rejecting it and then asking him to rework it all while apparently reducing the amount the studio would pay him for the script.[64] In the end, he was offered one thousand dollars for part of the script, a sum he had every intention of taking.[65] Boyd did have some luck during the summer. Paramount Pictures offered to pay him five hundred dollars a week for a few weeks' work on the script of *Come On, Marines!* which he worked on with screenwriter Jim McGuinness. In the end, none of his contributions were kept and he did not receive a screenwriting credit.[66] His career as a screenwriter was over. To make matters worse, he learned through F. Scott Fitzgerald one final piece of information that completed his disillusionment with Hollywood. In a 1930 letter to Max Perkins, Fitzgerald disclosed that another screenwriter and author, Lawrence Stallings, and director King Vidor had basically plagiarized *Through the Wheat* to create the battle scenes for the movie *The Big Parade*.[67] When Boyd learned of this plagiarism he thought of suing but was dissuaded by a lawyer who informed him of the long odds of winning such a case or of realizing any money from a legal action.[68]

Boyd's experience as a screenwriter disheartened him and had a negative impact on his career as an author. In addition to wasting a great deal of time in writing for the movies, his experience damaged his confidence. In a letter to Peggy he confided that he was unable to write anything other than the story he had prepared for the movies which he hoped to turn into a novel.[69] In fact, he had already forwarded a copy of the script to his agent Carl Brandt in New York in hopes of generating enough interest in the script as a story for serialization to warrant reworking it.[70] By the end of September, Boyd had conceived of and begun work on a novel that combined some of the characters of "The Wrong Diana" with the material that made up his screenplay. The story explored how the war destroyed the people whose lives it interrupted but resolved in a happy ending in which the two most sympathetic characters get together.[71] Perkins could not easily follow the plot of the novel from Boyd's letter, never having seen all the constituent parts together; but he advised Boyd to rewrite the material from the script before submitting it to *Scribner's* for a story contest and regular publication as Carl Brandt had advised.[72] Hopeful that Perkins's encouragement to rewrite the material meant that he had seen it and thought it worthy of publication, Boyd rewrote his script and submitted it to Scribner's through his agent. In truth, Perkins had not seen the manuscript and had encouraged Boyd to rewrite it only because he thought that it would have no chance of acceptance without being turned into standard prose.[73]

On November 6 through his agent Carl Brandt, Boyd received word from *Scribner's* editor Alfred Dashiell on the fate of his story:

> Both Perkins and I have read the Tom Boyd story, it does not seem to us adapted to the uses of the Magazine. As you know, war stuff is pretty much out unless it is something quite distinctive or some new method of treating it. There does not seem to be anything sufficiently distinctive in this story despite the fact that it is done with Boyd's fine skill.[74]

Perhaps sensing that the rejection would bring an angry response from Boyd, Perkins wrote to further explain why the story had been rejected. His letter probably only added to Boyd's confusion and anger.[75] Boyd, who had not responded to the letter from Dashiell, fired off an angry letter to Perkins:

> This present skirmish with Scribner's magazine is ending even more unpleasantly than the one before. . . . [N]ow according to Dashiell's letter to Carl Brandt, "Both Perkins and I" are of the opinion that "there does not seem to be anything sufficiently distinctive in this story" of Belleau Wood to warrant publication. And as I am planning this very material as the middle section of my next book, the above quoted judgment rather blows the ground from under me so far as Scribner's are concerned.
>
> Re-reading Dashiell's grammatical curiosity—"As you know, war stuff is pretty much out unless it is something quite distinctive or some new method of treating it."—I feel you should have discouraged Carl Brandt from submitting the manuscript.
>
> I am very grateful for all you have done for me and I vividly remember the thousand-dollar advance I had from Scribner's last spring. Perhaps the debt can be paid by money from my published books added to whatever I can send you from stories published later.[76]

Perkins's reply, like most of his replies to Boyd's angry letters, sought to explain what had happened; but this time he did not try to keep Boyd in the Scribner's fold and even allowed himself to display some irritation.[77] Boyd overcame his initial anger, but he must have realized that his relationship with Perkins and Scribner's had changed.

This argument with Scribner's, along with his failure in Hollywood and a period of serious illness for Ruth that concluded in surgery, led Boyd into a serious depression. His production as a writer dwindled to almost nothing, and for the first time he was forced to rely completely on Ruth's money for support. Under these circumstances, he and Ruth returned to New England to live in Vermont. From his home in Vermont he would make his last attempts to write for a mass audience, and he would formally embrace the radical politics he had been moving toward for most of his life.

chapter eight

"I think there will be a revolution in this country . . ."

DESPITE REALIZING HIS desire to settle in Vermont, Thomas Boyd's years there were not entirely happy ones. His dependence on his wife's money irritated him and in order to earn his own living he developed several ideas for novels, revived his working relationship with his ex-wife, and found a new publisher. His professional frustrations also led him to embrace communism fully and to make a brief foray into politics. With all his professional disappointments and outside interests, the Vermont years were, in the sense of finding and making a home, some of the most personally stable years of his life. But his personal life was the source of serious concerns and his professional life fell apart. The added stress he placed on himself to solve these problems only worsened his fragile health and contributed to his untimely death.

On their way from California to Vermont, the Boyds stopped in Ridgefield to see Betty Grace and Peggy and to stretch their legs. Tom and Peggy had a brief, heated conversation before he and Ruth continued their trip. Once in Vermont, they set up camp at the White Cupboard Inn in Woodstock. Real estate was scarce and expensive in Woodstock itself, but they found a house that they had seen before and which met all of Boyd's requirements for an ideal home in nearby South Woodstock.[1] The house was built before 1816 and overlooked the Kedron River valley from a lot set back off a narrow country lane.[2]

Once settled in South Woodstock, Boyd turned his attention toward once again becoming a provider for his family and a publishing author. Having to live off his wife's wealth for a few months was having an effect on his self-esteem and his marriage. In a letter to Peggy he confided these feelings and his concerns about the future of his marriage:

> The main trouble is this: I don't know how long I can go on living in this way, with Ruth as a protective featherbed and myself as a surly hound that wont lie still. . . . Up until last February I contributed my quota of the general expense, but then I dropped and since then I've earned nothing. . . . Now you can guess and I don't have to guess how badly I need to get started again and what I've been seriously thinking is this: If you think it would work out and were willing to do it, I might go to the neighborhood of Ridgefield . . . and there take up the practice we had four years ago—of your writing synopses and my expanding them for the pulps—until I got enough money and confidence to write novels again. . . . Ever since summer I have made it plain to Ruth that I think she and Walter ought to live together again. They are both devoted to the boys and I know Walter would welcome the chance to remarry Ruth. But as long as I'm around she won't consider it.
>
> That's the whole story. I'm not in a hurry to do anything about it; I'm not driven by any immediate desire; there's nothing desperate at all about it except that I've got to be able to conceive of myself as a self respecting, self supporting person sometime fairly soon and that such a vision, with large expenses going on continuously is denied me here.

> Please think about all this and then let me know. It may sound fantastic of me to be writing it to you, but after all, no matter how lousy I was, we both must have kept some sympathy for each other out of our breakup.[3]

Though it is unclear exactly what Boyd was asking Peggy, they did retain real feelings for one another. In the years that Tom and Ruth lived in South Woodstock, he and Peggy would attempt to resume their working relationship and once again become confidants.

Though Boyd was eager to renew his working arrangements with Peggy, his first hopes for publication and income lay with Scribner's and Max Perkins. Before leaving Hollywood, Boyd had completed a novel which he titled "A Wall Like China's." The plot followed closely the story of his marriage to Peggy.

> It is a simple story of two people who marry, are in love with each other, but get driven apart by circumstances over which they have no control till finally, though all their intentions have been good, they end in tragedy, but still in love.[4]

Boyd sent the novel to Perkins as soon as it was completed sometime near the end of September 1932.[5] Perkins rejected the novel on the grounds that the book would not generate enough interest to achieve an adequate sale.[6] Despite this, Perkins's letter, as his previous correspondence had always been, was encouraging. A few months earlier he had proposed a scheme by which Boyd could get an advance on an historical novel and use his royalties to pay back the thousand dollars he still owed Scribner's.[7] Though in need of money and a fresh start, Boyd hesitated to agree: "With such a strong feeling of how cockeyed the world is, it will be a horrible admission of my incompetence if I can't write anything but a historical novel."[8]

Despite serious reservations, Boyd's financial situation was such that he sought to get reinstatement for compensation from the Veterans Bureau. Since his return to the United States following the war, Boyd's health had often caused him problems and the damage done to his lungs and throat by the gas attack at Mont Blanc made him eligible for compensation.[9] His application for reinstatement was eventually approved, but his compensation checks were too small to be of much help. Boyd received only $14.25 a month, an amount that was more insulting than helpful.[10]

In 1933, Boyd and Peggy did begin writing stories for pulp magazines—Peggy outlining stories and Tom fleshing out the details.[11] While these projects provided Boyd with his own income, they did not give him the financial independence he desired. In defeat he wrote Perkins to ask if Scribner's would still be interested in an historical novel and if an arrangement could be made whereby he would receive money from its sale rather than having his royalties applied to his debt.[12] When Perkins assured him that such an arrangement could be made, Boyd began work on the novel.[13] But his heart was not in the work. A letter to Peggy showed just how low his spirits and his opinion of himself had sunk:

> I never set up to be a historian—nor very seriously as a biographer. However, I think if you went about asking novelists if I were a good novelist, short story writers if I were a good writer of stories, essayists if I could write essays, biographers if I were a good biographer, etc. I think you would find each of them would say I was pretty damned lousy and that I should have stuck to newspaper work—where I was equally poor.[14]

Returning to the opinion he had of his writing ability when he and Peggy were first married, he naturally looked to her for reassurance. Nothing he did gave him any passion for writing the historical novel. But other passions, political passions, replaced his authorial passion and subsumed his financial worries.

By the end of 1933, Thomas Boyd had become deeply immersed in the radical politics that proliferated during the Great Depression, and he was openly rejecting the capitalist system. Hints of Boyd's conversion began to show up in his correspondence with Max Perkins. In an April 1934 letter, Boyd wrote that he was abandoning plans to write a historical novel and instead was reworking the manuscript of "A Wall Like China's." He was adding new material to the manuscript and attempting "to give all of it an economic significance."[15] By the end of April, Boyd had completed his changes and began trying to convince Perkins to publish it. He personally delivered the manuscript to Perkins at the end of April, hoping to get a quick decision so that he could place the novel with another publisher if Scribner's rejected it.[16] His answer came quickly. On May 17 Perkins wrote to inform him that Scribner's would not be publishing the novel, now entitled "Trampled Grain."[17] Boyd did not respond for several months. When he did, he firmly stated his intention to write novels of historical and economic importance with or without the support of Perkins and Scribner's:

> I've been meaning to write you and thank you for your last letter; but there really isn't much more than that for me to say.
>
> Whether I'll ever be able to write an historical novel or a biography that Scribner's will want to publish is one of those confounded questions. I was extremely disappointed when you rejected the novel—whether you were justified in your attitude has yet to be seen. I am now writing the Fitch biography for Putnam, who will publish the novel in January. Frankly, I don't care much for Earle and Minton, but so long as they will publish my books I can't ask any more.
>
> But no matter what happens, whether I get published or not, whether capitalism temporarily jerks out of the crisis or not, I'll never write again without a definite point of view. And that point of view must always be unpopular to people who can afford to buy books under present conditions. I never wanted much from the old set-up, but I was denied what little I did want. I'm glad that so far as I'm concerned it's gone, for I feel at last that I'm going forward not retreating as I tried so long and so unsuccessfully to do.[18]

Boyd's letter signified the end of his relationship with Scribner's and his professional relationship with Max Perkins. It also signaled his break with traditional American political ideas and a shift in the way he thought about himself. Boyd no longer thought of himself as an honest, hardworking writer hoping to score a big success, but as the victim of an unfair and corrupt system that was finally collapsing.

To friends like Perkins, who had lived some distance from Boyd for many years, his conversion to a Marxist view of society may have seemed sudden. But to those closest to him and those with whom he communicated regularly the change probably seemed a long time in the making.

From his willing indoctrination into Christian Science and his eager acceptance of the ethics of the Marine Corps, Boyd had often embraced value systems outside the mainstream. In fact, he had dabbled in socialism and communism since he had followed Peggy from Chicago to Minnesota and met her father. Boyd's writing often reflected his left-of-center beliefs. In the introduction to his collection of short stories, Boyd blamed the financiers and corporations that profited from the First World War for starting the war. And his best short stories were usually those in which he depicted the underdog in society—whether his grandfather or an escaped convict—coming up against the power of the established interests in society. Only after the collapse of the American economy in 1929 and the resulting collapse of the market for books did Boyd fully embrace communism.

In a letter to his mother written more than a year before his break with Scribner's, Boyd expressed a clear sense of the economic catastrophe he believed capitalism had brought about:

> I'm sorry you got that little slip in your pay envelope instead of money, but the same thing is happening everywhere and at least fifteen million people in this country haven't enough to eat. And under these circumstances I think we're both comparatively well off.
>
> How long the people will put up with it I don't know, but it seems to me we'll have to have a change in our form of government before we'll get anywhere. From all I can find out the people of Russia are much better off basically than we are.[19]

By the time Franklin Roosevelt had been inaugurated and the New Deal implemented, Boyd was convinced that American capitalism was coming to an end; and he had decided to do something to help it along. In a 1933 letter to Peggy he wrote, "I think there will be a revolution in this country and while I don't want to be the leader of it I certainly don't want to stand on the sidelines and give a feeble cheer."[20] Always a man of action, Boyd joined a local Communist Party chapter and began to work earnestly to promote communist causes in the United States.

For Ruth Boyd, her husband's decision to become a communist seemed like a product of his background and his professional disappointments. She did not feel that his conversion was the result of deep study or even deep thinking, but rather an emotional response to the difficulty he had getting his books published and his experiences in Hollywood; furthermore, the fact that the only books on economic theory he had ever read were books that outlined communist and socialist principles made Ruth doubt the depths of his commitment to the communist cause.[21] As the daughter of a banker and the product of privilege, Ruth must have been unsettled by Boyd's conversion to communism, and she never fully credited his decision to become a communist to anything other than the hard times in which he lived. Regardless of the reasons for his conversion, Boyd's commitment to the party was genuine and his desire to do something to make a difference, sincere.[22]

Boyd's first act to promote the cause of communism in the United States was his most significant. The Communist Party of Vermont wanted to place the name of one of its members on the ballot in the gubernatorial election of 1934. They wanted a candidate that represented a typical American, and Boyd with his good looks and plain name was their first choice.

Though uncomfortable as a public speaker, Boyd accepted the nomination and set out to collect the signatures necessary to get his name on the ballot. He crisscrossed Vermont speaking and collecting signatures.[23] Granville Hicks, a leader within the Communist Party in the United States and the editor of the *New Masses*, accompanied Boyd on one of his trips and spoke with him at rallies in Barre and Bennington. Hicks's account makes it clear that Boyd was a poor speaker, but that because he was motivated by an honest belief in what he was saying, he could be effective, particularly when addressing crowds of workers.[24] Despite his shortcomings as a speaker, Boyd succeeded in collecting the fifteen hundred signatures he needed to become the first Communist Party candidate for governor in the history of Vermont.

The actual campaign for governor was perfunctory and unsuccessful. Boyd continued to travel the state and speak in support of his candidacy, and some campaign literature was circulated. One flyer printed by the Communist Party's New England District carried the headline "Vote Communist! For Governor Thomas Boyd" complete with a hammer and sickle. Boyd's platform included a call for relief efforts to help farmers, those in danger of losing their homes, and those who had lost money in banks that had gone out of business; and it advocated the passage of the Workers Unemployment Insurance Bill, which would have paid unemployed workers eighteen dollars a week.[25] In the end, Boyd's ideas and his sincerity were of little help. In the November election he received fewer than one thousand votes.

Fortunately Boyd had not placed any hope in being elected governor. Instead, he had spent much of 1934 preparing two manuscripts for publication by Minton Balch Putnam. Both had been rejected by Scribner's, and both represented a clear attempt on Boyd's part to advance communist beliefs through literature.

The first, *In Time of Peace,* was published in February 1935. The novel picked up the story of William Hicks, the protagonist of *Through the Wheat,* after his return from the Great War and followed him through his first jobs, the courtship of his wife, marriage, an affair, and a loss of faith in capitalism. Just as *Through the Wheat* had been a fictionalized version of Boyd's own experiences in the First World War, *In Time of Peace* was a fictionalized version of Boyd's life since his own return. More important to Boyd at the time, the new novel carried the communist message throughout its pages. Near the end of the book, Hicks has an epiphany about the evils of the capitalist system after being shot while protesting a factory closing:

> Lying on the pavement, he gasped from sheer disbelief. He was an American citizen protesting against intolerable conditions into

> which he had found himself being forced. No more than that. And he had been clipped by a machine gun bullet when there was no chance of his fighting back. If he had had a gun he could have understood it, but he had been shot down by a man he had never threatened, by a man he had never seen before. . . .
>
> Then the numbness left. Pain rushed with air into his wound—hot, exquisite stabs of violence. His chin dropped, waggling from self pity. But no, by God! Back of the guards stood the police and back of the police the politicians . . . and behind them all the sacred name of property. In the name of property he could be starved to death, and if they so much as raised their heads, there was war. Hicks gritted his teeth. If it was war again, he was glad to know it. He at least had something to fight for now.[26]

Boyd no doubt hoped that *In Time of Peace* would be his first contribution to the fight against capitalism and entrenched property interests. As an impassioned piece of propaganda the novel succeeded in communicating its message, but as a work of fiction it had serious shortcomings.

Book critics did not think much of *In Time of Peace*. The reviewer for the *Nation* wrote:

> It is unusual to find a proletarian novel which is not violent enough for the most sensational taste. Yet it must be confessed that 'In Time of Peace,' Thomas Boyd's latest work, is too placid to realize the revolutionary intent. . . . Mr. Boyd's novel for all its seriousness of purpose falls into the large and useless class of plodding, studiously life like, novels, which are read to pass the time away, and whose scenes and characters are so well padded with comfortable verbal realism that they are easily forgotten.[27]

Even Boyd's friend and fellow communist Granville Hicks admitted that *In Time of Peace* failed as a novel and as a piece of propaganda.[28] If American reviewers and communists thought little of *In Time of Peace*, there were those in Russia who had positive feelings for both the book and its author.

On September 6, Mary Reed, an American working for the Soviet publisher Gosizdat, wrote American Comintern representative Pat Toohey to find out if Boyd was a good communist and, therefore, if it were safe to publish *In Time of Peace* in the Soviet Union.[29] Ms. Toohey wrote back reassuring Ms. Reed that Boyd met the standard necessary for publication: "[H]e was a communist and promising revolutionary writer."[30]

Boyd also completed work on the biography of John Fitch that he had been working on and trying to place with Scribner's for some time. Published a few months after *In Time of Peace*, *Poor John Fitch, Inventor of the Steamboat* was a biography with a purpose. That purpose gave the book a force that some of his other books sometimes lacked. The biography followed the life of John Fitch from his days as an American soldier during the Revolutionary War through his successful attempts to construct a steam-powered boat and his unsuccessful attempt to secure protection and credit for his invention. The book's point of view is decidedly communist. Through his research Boyd concluded that Fitch was denied his rightful place in history and the money that went with it because powerful members of the Potomac Company—men like George Washington and Thomas Jefferson—saw his invention and its practical application on the Ohio and Mississippi as a threat to their plans to develop the upper Potomac as the trade route from the Alleghenies.[31] Whether his conclusions were well supported in the biography, *Poor John Fitch* did help resurrect Fitch's claim to be the true inventor of the steamboat.

For Thomas Boyd, 1934 was a busy and eventful year but not always a happy one. His relationship with Ruth continued to suffer from his inability to earn a living for himself and his resentment of living off her money. More than once he wrote Peggy to ask if she could help him relocate to the Ridgefield area.[32] When Peggy and her new husband Ted Shane decided to try their luck in Hollywood and moved to California, they allowed Tom and Ruth to move in to the Ridgefield house to look after Betty Grace.

Boyd's health failed completely in January 1935. The first signs of the end came during the second week of January while Boyd was in New York meeting with his new publisher. He suffered what was later described as a slight stroke while riding in a cab. He spent several days in the hospital under observation before returning to Ridgefield in an extremely weakened condition.[33] On January 26, Boyd wrote Peggy to tell her what had happened and to reassure her:

> The trouble with me is glandular, which affected my circulation and which knocked me out completely the day I reached New York. I was five days in the hospital and even now I only get up in the afternoon. But I will be alright so don't worry.[34]

On the morning of January 27, 1935, Peggy's father, Duncan Smith, who had relocated to Ridgefield, sat down to write a letter about Boyd's health and his own situation:

> Dear Margaret: I got your air mail letter yesterday. I called up the house and they [the Boyds] invited me to dinner. I called again this morning and Tom had had another bad spell. He was in bed under the care of a doctor and a nurse and no one could see him. So I didn't go out. I will call again in the morning before I mail this. . . .[35]

The letter went on to describe the New York episode, the weather, and his new living arrangements and was signed in preparation for mailing. But before it was mailed, a handwritten message was added:

> The funeral will be at the Episcopal Church Tuesday afternoon.
>
> Alice [Boyd's mother] came this morning. I haven't seen her yet.
>
> I held this to get more information as they told me they had notified you by telegraph. New York papers gave it much space.[36]

Thomas Boyd had died of a cerebral hemorrhage at approximately 9:30 in the morning on January 27, 1935, at the age of thirty-six.[37] Veterans Administration doctors later concluded that the gassing Boyd received during the First World War contributed to the condition that led to his death.[38]

Boyd's daughter, Betty Grace, remembered one of her last conversations with her father in great detail:

> I remember one morning he called me into his room and gave me "In Time of Peace"; showing me the dedication [To Betty Grace Boyd]; very proud of the book I thought. It was a bright sunny morning and the room had lots of windows and he seemed extra alive and vital.[39]

Her description of him on one of his last days captured the essence of Boyd's life; always intensely active and committed to working hard and always hopeful that he was on the verge of another major success. Perhaps it was appropriate for him to die suddenly and at a young age.

In his short life, Thomas Boyd experienced more of the tumult and change that the United States went through in the first third of the twentieth century than any other writer of the "lost generation" and most people alive during the time period. Driven by a desire to succeed and a desire for acceptance, Boyd pushed himself through a life of accomplishments and change. Boyd's vitality and passion for the things that interested him inform his published works. From the autobiographical *Through the Wheat* to his biography of John Fitch, Boyd wrote about men of action, men who took risks, and men who oftentimes failed to achieve greatness through no fault of their own. Boyd was not the greatest literary artist of his generation. As he himself admitted, he was better at explaining things than inventing them. Though Boyd is a minor figure in American literary history, *Through the Wheat* remains one of the finest American war novels ever written and his Ohio novels and biographies reflect the burgeoning pride Americans had in their history during the 1920s and 1930s. In addition, his life represents the period in which he lived and reflects the best and the worst of America in the decades following the beginning of the twentieth century.

Chronology of Thomas Boyd's Published Works

1920

November 21– First edition of In a Corner with the Bookworm appears in the *St. Paul Daily News*

1922

March 5, 12, 19 – "Literary Libels: Francis Scott Key Fitzgerald," *St. Paul Daily News*

March 26, April 2, 9 – "Literary Libels: Carl Sandburg," *St. Paul Daily News*

April 30 – "Literary Libels: Witter Bynner," *St. Paul Daily News*

1923

April – *Through the Wheat* published by Charles Scribner's Sons

1924

April – "Rintintin," *Scribner's*

May – "Unadorned," *Scribner's*

July – "Sound Adjutants Call," *Scribner's*

September – *The Dark Cloud* published by Charles Scribner's Sons

November – "The Uninvited," *American Mercury*

December – "Semper Fidelis," *Bookman*

1925

January – "The Kentucky Boy," *Scribner's*

February – "A Little Gall," *Scribner's*

March – "Responsibility," *Scribner's*
Points of Honor published by Charles Scribner's Sons
August – *Samuel Drummond* published by Charles Scribner's Sons
December – "An Ohio Fable," *Scribner's*

1926

January – "Good Roads," *Scribner's*
March – "My Favorite Fictional Character," *Bookman*
July – "Defying the Klan," *Forum*
August – "The Salt of the Earth," *Scribner's*
December – "The Fighting Face," *Short Stories*

1927

January – "The Bibliophile," *Bookman*
February – "Dark in a Shell Hole," *Short Stories*
May – "Lugubrious Luke," *Popular Magazine*
July – "Grandfather's Dog," *Scribner's*
October – "A Bow to Progress," *Scribner's*

1928

April – "Take His Name Sergeant," *Popular Magazine*
May – *Shadow of the Long Knives* published by Charles Scribner's Sons
"Our Top Sergeant," *Scribner's*
August – *Simon Girty: The White Savage* published by Minton Balch and Company
September – "When a Princess Commands," *Scribner's*
November – "Sounds Out of Darkness," *Popular Magazine*

1929

June – with Woodward Boyd, "Diversey 4932," *Popular Magazine*
August – with Woodward Boyd, "The Veiled Ruler of Ghazale," *Popular Magazine*
October – *Mad Anthony Wayne* published by Charles Scribner's Sons

November – "Mayor of Benbury," *Woman's Home Companion*
with Woodward Boyd, "The Beer Runners," *Popular Magazine*

1930

February – "Bloodhounds," *Atlantic Monthly*
"Love in the Wilderness," *North American Review*
March – "Extreme Mental Cruelty," *Ladies' Home Journal*
August – "A Resident of Purgatory," *Harper's*

1931

April – "Bright Faced Danger," *Colliers*
Light Horse Harry Lee published by Charles Scribner's Sons

1935

February – *In Time of Peace* published by Minton Balch and Company (posthumous)
April – *Poor John Fitch, Inventor of the Steamboat* published by G. P. Putnam's Sons (posthumous)

1978

Through the Wheat with afterword by James Dickey, published by Southern Illinois University Press

2000

Through the Wheat with an introduction by Edwin Howard Simmons, published by University of Nebraska Press

Notes

Abbreviations
ADB: Alice Dunbar Boyd
EGB: Elizabeth Grace Boyd
FSF: F. Scott Fitzgerald
MP: Maxwell Perkins
PB: Margaret "Peggy" Boyd
RFB: Ruth Fitch Boyd
TB: Thomas Boyd

Chapter 1

1. Elizabeth Grace Boyd, untitled biography of Thomas Boyd (senior thesis, Vassar College, 1943), 1–15; ADB to EGB, November 17, 1942, Mss 1269 AV, Thomas Boyd Papers, Ohio Historical Society.

2. Elizabeth Grace Boyd, 1–4.

3. ADB to EGB, 1943, Mss 1269 AV, Thomas Boyd Papers, Ohio Historical Society.

4. Elizabeth Grace Boyd, 9–13.

5. Ibid., 14–24.

6. ADB to EGB, 1943, Mss 1269 AV, Thomas Boyd Papers, Ohio Historical Society.

7. TB to ADB, April 20, 1917, Mss 1269 AV, Thomas Boyd Papers, Ohio Historical Society.

8. Elizabeth Grace Boyd, 24–30.

9. TB to ADB, March 12, 1917, Mss 1269 AV, Thomas Boyd Papers, Ohio Historical Society.

10. TB to ADB, c. 1917, Mss 1269 AV, Thomas Boyd Papers, Ohio Historical Society.

11. TB to ADB, c. 1916, Mss 1269 AV, Thomas Boyd Papers, Ohio Historical Society.

12. TB to ADB, April 20, 1917, Mss 1269 AV, Thomas Boyd Papers, Ohio Historical Society.

13. Margaret Shane to Granville Hicks, November 25, 1941, Papers of Granville Hicks, Department of Special Collections, Syracuse University Libraries.

14. Elizabeth Grace Boyd, 32.

15. TB to ADB, c. April 1917, Mss 1269 AV, Thomas Boyd Papers, Ohio Historical Society.

16. TB to ADB, c. April 1917, Mss 1269 AV, Thomas Boyd Papers, Ohio Historical Society.

17. TB to ADB, May 20, 1917, Mss 1269 AV, Thomas Boyd Papers, Ohio Historical Society.

Chapter 2

1. Lieutenant General William K. Jones, *A Brief History of the 6th Marines* (Washington, D.C.: History and Museums Division Headquarters, U.S. Marine Corps, 1987), 1.

2. TB to ADB, May 26, 1917, Mss 1269 AV, Thomas Boyd Papers, Ohio Historical Society.

3. TB to ADB, c. August 1917, Mss 1269 AV, Thomas Boyd Papers, Ohio Historical Society.

4. TB to ADB, c. July 17, 1917, Mss 1269 AV, Thomas Boyd Papers, Ohio Historical Society.

5. TB to ADB, c. July 24, 1917, Mss 1269 AV, Thomas Boyd Papers, Ohio Historical Society.

6. TB to Marion Wilde, September 13, 1917, Mss 1269 AV, Thomas Boyd Papers, Ohio Historical Society.

7. Military Record of Thomas Alexander Boyd, Mss 1269 AV, Thomas Boyd Papers, Ohio Historical Society.

8. Jones, *6th Marines*, 2.

9. TB to ADB, c. March 1918, Mss 1269 AV, Thomas Boyd Papers, Ohio Historical Society.

10. Thomas Boyd, *Through the Wheat* (New York: Scribner's, 1923), 1–2.

11. Elizabeth Grace Boyd, 35–36.

12. Jones, *6th Marines*, 3.

13. Boyd, *Through the Wheat*, 21–23.

14. Jones, *6th Marines*, 3–5.

15. Lawrence Stallings, *The Doughboys* (New York: Harper and Row, 1963), 77–80.

16. Dale Van Every, *The A.E.F. in Battle* (New York: D. Appleton and Company, 1928), 51–53.

17. Boyd, *Through the Wheat*, 65.

18. Van Every, *A.E.F*, 57–58.

19. Boyd, *Through the Wheat*, 78–79.

20. Ibid., 83.

21. Van Every, *A.E.F.*, 61–71.

22. Jones, *6th Marines*, 6–10.

23. Boyd, *Through the Wheat*, 107.

24. Jones, *6th Marines*, 10–13.

25. Van Every, *A.E.F.*, 128.

26. Jones, *6th Marines*, 13–14.

27. Boyd, *Through the Wheat*, 186–92.

28. Jones, *6th Marines*, 14.

29. Edwin Howard Simmons, introduction to *Through the Wheat* by Thomas Boyd (Lincoln: Bison Books/University of Nebraska Press, 2000), xi–xii.

30. Boyd, *Through the Wheat*, 155–60.

31. Ibid., 210.

32. Jones, *6th Marines*, 15.

33. Van Every, *A.E.F.*, 283–88.

34. Military Record of Thomas Boyd, Mss 1269 AV, Thomas Boyd Papers, Ohio Historical Society.

35. Thomas Boyd, "The Long Shot," story in *Points of Honor* (New York: Charles Scribner's Sons, 1925), 257.

36. The Board of Veterans Appeals, Boyd, Thomas A., XC-507, 735, August 31, 1939, Mss 1269 AV, Thomas Boyd Papers, Ohio Historical Society.

37. TB to ADB, October 27, 1918, Mss 1269 AV, Thomas Boyd Papers, Ohio Historical Society.

38. TB to ADB, December 22, 1918, Mss 1269 AV, Thomas Boyd Papers, Ohio Historical Society.

39. TB to ADB, c. October 1918, The Personal Collection of Brainerd F. Phillipson.

40. Military Record of Thomas Boyd, The Board of Veterans Appeals, Mss 1269 AV, Thomas Boyd Papers, Ohio Historical Society.

41. Boyd, *Through the Wheat*, 263–66.

Chapter 3

1. Elizabeth Grace Boyd, 38–40.

2. Thomas Boyd, *In Time of Peace* (New York: Minton Balch Putnam, 1935), 8–9.

3. Elizabeth Grace Boyd, 40–48.

4. Peggy Smith to TB, c. 1920, Mss 1269 AV, Thomas Boyd Papers, Ohio Historical Society.

5. Elizabeth Grace Boyd, 49–50.

6. Margaret Shane to Granville Hicks, November 25, 1941, Papers of Granville Hicks, Department of Special Collections, Syracuse University Libraries.

7. Elizabeth Grace Boyd, 50–59.

8. Boyd, *In Time of Peace*, 56.

9. Elizabeth Grace Boyd, 60–75.

10. Thomas Boyd, In a Corner with the Bookworm, *St. Paul Daily News*, September 17, 1922, City Life section, p. 6.

11. Thomas Boyd, In a Corner with the Bookworm, *St. Paul Daily News*, March 20, 1921, City Life section, p. 6.

12. Thomas Boyd, In a Corner with the Bookworm, *St. Paul Daily News*, March 26, 1921, City Life section, p. 6.

13. Thomas Boyd, In a Corner with the Bookworm, *St. Paul Daily News*, February 26, 1922, City Life section, p. 6.

14. FSF to TB, February 9, 1921, F. Scott Fitzgerald Additional Papers, Manuscripts Division, Department of Rare Books and Special Collections, Princeton University Library. Published with permission of the Princeton University Library.

15. Charles Norris to TB, published in In a Corner with the Bookworm, *St. Paul Daily News*, November 6, 1921, City Life section, p. 6.

16. Sinclair Lewis to TB, published in In a Corner with the Bookworm, *St. Paul Daily News*, October 15, 1922, City Life section, p. 6.

17. Thomas Boyd, "Sinclair Lewis' Last Novel," published in In a Corner with the Bookworm, *St. Paul Daily News*, September 17, 1922, City Life section, p. 6.

18. Thomas Boyd, "A Mental Vivisectionist," published in In a Corner with the Bookworm, *St. Paul Daily News*, October 8, 1922, City Life section, p. 6.

19. Thomas Boyd, "Literary Libels: Carl Sandburg," *St. Paul Daily News*, March 26, April 2 and 9, 1922, City Life section, p. 6.

20. Matthew J. Bruccoli, *Some Sort of Epic Grandeur: The Life of F. Scott Fitzgerald* (New York: Carroll & Graf, 1993), 176.

21. Elizabeth Grace Boyd, 69–74.

22. Thomas Boyd, "Literary Libels: F. Scott Fitzgerald," *St. Paul Daily News*, March 5, 12, and 19, 1922, City Life section, p. 6.

23. Cornelius Van Ness to Granville Hicks, January 15, 1942, Papers of Granville Hicks, Department of Special Collections, Syracuse University Libraries.

24. Bruccoli, *Some Sort of Epic Grandeur*, 179.

25. Elizabeth Grace Boyd, 71.

26. FSF to MP, c. February 10, 1922, in *Dear Scott/Dear Max: The Fitzgerald-Perkins Correspondence*, ed. John Kuehl and Jackson R. Bryer (New York: Charles Scribner's Sons, 1971), 55–56.

27. Elizabeth Grace Boyd, 46.

28. FSF to PB, c. 1922, Mss 1269 AV, Thomas Boyd Papers, Ohio Historical Society.

29. MP to PB, March 10, 1922, the Archives of Charles Scribner's Sons, Manuscripts Division, Department of Rare Books and Special Collections, Princeton University Library.

30. PB to TB, c. June 1922; TB to PB, c. June 1922, Mss 1269 AV, Thomas Boyd Papers, Ohio Historical Society.

31. PB to MP, c. June 13, 1922, the Archives of Charles Scribner's Sons, Manuscripts Division, Department of Rare Books and Special Collections, Princeton University Library.

32. MP to PB, June 13, 1922, the Archives of Charles Scribner's Sons, Manuscripts Division, Department of Rare Books and Special Collections, Princeton University Library.

33. PB to TB, c. 1922, Mss 1269 AV, Thomas Boyd Papers, Ohio Historical Society.

34. MP to TB, September 1, 1922, the Archives of Charles Scribner's Sons, Manuscripts Division, Department of Rare Books and Special Collections, Princeton University Library.

35. F. Scott Fitzgerald, "A Rugged Novel," review of *The Love Legend* by Woodward Boyd, *Literary Review: New York Evening Post*, October 28, 1922.

36. "Woodward Boyd's *The Love Legend*," *New York Times*, October 28, 1922.

37. Review of *The Love Legend*, *Chicago Daily News*, November 8, 1922.

38. Sinclair Lewis to PB, December 28, 1922, The Personal Collection of Brainerd F. Phillipson.

39. Elizabeth Grace Boyd, 80–87.

40. Margaret Shane to Granville Hicks, November 25, 1941, Papers of Granville Hicks, Department of Special Collections, Syracuse University Libraries. TB to PB, c. June 1922, Mss 1269 AV, Thomas Boyd Papers, Ohio Historical Society.

41. Elizabeth Grace Boyd, 89–90.

42. Cornelius Van Ness to EGB, c. 1943, The Personal Collection of Brainerd F. Phillipson.

43. Harrison Smith to TB, August 18, 1922, Mss 1269 AV, Thomas Boyd Papers, Ohio Historical Society.

44. Sinclair Lewis to MP, December 11, 1922, the Archives of Charles Scribner's Sons, Manuscripts Division, Department of Rare Books and Special Collections, Princeton University Library.

45. Harrison Smith to TB, September 14, 1922, The Personal Collection of Brainerd F. Phillipson.

46. MP to TB, October 4, 1922, the Archives of Charles Scribner's Sons, Manuscripts Division, Department of Rare Books and Special Collections, Princeton University Library.

47. TB to MP, November 13, 1922, the Archives of Charles Scribner's Sons, Manuscripts Division, Department of Rare Books and Special Collections, Princeton University Library. Published with permission of the Princeton University Library.

48. Elizabeth Grace Boyd, 81.

49. Ibid., 81–91.

50. Boyd, *In Time of Peace*, 131.

51. Bruccoli, *Some Sort of Epic Grandeur*, 176–77, 202.

52. Charles Flandrau to TB, December 29, 1922, Papers of Charles Macomb Flandrau, Department of Special Collections, Beinecke Library, Harvard University.

53. FSF to TB, c. October 1922, The Personal Collection of Brainerd F. Phillipson.

54. FSF and MP to TB, December 13, 1922, The Personal Collection of Brainerd F. Phillipson.

55. FSF to TB, c. December 13, 1922, The Personal Collection of Brainerd F. Phillipson.

56. Bruccoli, *Some Sort of Epic Grandeur*, 178; FSF to MP, c. March 15, 1926, in Bruccoli, *F. Scott Fitzgerald: A Life in Letters*, 140.

57. FSF to MP, c. February 10, 1922, in Kuehl and Bryer, *Dear Scott/Dear Max*, 55–56.

58. Bruccoli, *Some Sort of Epic Grandeur*, 106.

59. TB to FSF, c. December 1922, Papers of F. Scott Fitzgerald, Manuscripts Division, Department of Rare Books and Special Collections, Princeton University Library. Published with permission of the Princeton University Library.

Chapter 4

1. FSF to TB, c. December 1922, Papers of F. Scott Fitzgerald, Manuscripts Division, Department of Rare Books and Special Collections, Princeton University Library. Published with permission of the Princeton University Library.

2. TB to MP, January 15 and 23, 1923, the Archives of Charles Scribner's Sons, Manuscripts Division, Department of Rare Books and Special Collections, Princeton University Library.

3. MP to TB, March 3, 1923, the Archives of Charles Scribner's Sons, Manuscripts Division, Department of Rare Books and Special Collections, Princeton University Library.

4. TB to MP, March 7, 1923, the Archives of Charles Scribner's Sons, Manuscripts Division, Department of Rare Books and Special Collections, Princeton University Library. Published with permission of the Princeton University Library.

5. TB to MP, March 12, 1923, and MP to TB, March 16, 1923, the Archives of Charles Scribner's Sons, Manuscripts Division, Department of Rare Books and Special Collections, Princeton University Library. Published with permission of the Princeton University Library.

6. Ibid.; TB to MP, c. March 20, 1923, the Archives of Charles Scribner's Sons, Manuscripts Division, Department of Rare Books and Special Collections, Princeton University Library.

7. TB to MP, March 4, 1923, the Archives of Charles Scribner's Sons, Manuscripts Division, Department of Rare Books and Special Collections, Princeton University Library.

8. MP to Edmund Wilson, April 3, 1923, the Archives of Charles Scribner's Sons, Manuscripts Division, Department of Rare Books and Special Collections, Princeton University Library. Published with permission of the Princeton University Library.

9. MP to TB, April 24, 1923, the Archives of Charles Scribner's Sons, Manuscripts Division, Department of Rare Books and Special Collections, Princeton University Library.

10. A. Scott Berg, *Max Perkins: Editor of Genius* (New York: Riverhead Books/The Berkeley Publishing Group, 1978), 56.

11. F. Scott Fitzgerald, "Under Fire," review of *Through the Wheat* by Thomas Boyd, *Literary Review: New York Evening Post*, May 26, 1923, 715.

12. Theodore Dreiser to TB, June 9, 1923, The Personal Collection of Brainerd F. Phillipson.

13. John W. Crawford, "A Malicious Panorama," review of *Through the Wheat* by Thomas Boyd, *Nation* 117 (May 1923): 66.

14. Edmund Wilson, review of *Through the Wheat* by Thomas Boyd, *Dial* (July, 1923): 93–95.

15. "Latest Works of Fiction," review of *Through the Wheat*, by Thomas Boyd, *New York Times Book Review*, April 29, 1923, 14.

16. Brent G. Nunnaly to Charles Scribner's Sons, May 19, 1923, the Archives of Charles Scribner's Sons, Manuscripts Division, Department of Rare Books and Special Collections, Princeton University Library. Published with permission of the Princeton University Library.

17. TB to MP, c. March 25, 1924, the Archives of Charles Scribner's Sons, Manuscripts Division, Department of Rare Books and Special Collections, Princeton University Library. Published with permission of the Princeton University Library.

18. Lieutenant Colonel John Hughes to MP, June 1, 1923, the Archives of Charles Scribner's Sons, Manuscripts Division, Department of Rare Books and Special Collections, Princeton University Library.

19. MP to TB, June 11, 1923, the Archives of Charles Scribner's Sons, Manuscripts Division, Department of Rare Books and Special Collections, Princeton University Library. Published with permission of the Princeton University Library.

20. Ibid.

21. MP to PB, June 20 and July 10, 1923, the Archives of Charles Scribner's Sons, Manuscripts Division, Department of Rare Books and Special Collections, Princeton University Library.

22. TB to MP, April 28, 1923, the Archives of Charles Scribner's Sons, Manuscripts Division, Department of Rare Books and Special Collections, Princeton University Library. Published with permission of the Princeton University Library.

23. Elizabeth Grace Boyd, 90.

24. MP to PB, August 6, 1923, the Archives of Charles Scribner's Sons, Manuscripts Division, Department of Rare Books and Special Collections, Princeton University Library.

25. MP to PB, July 24, 1923, the Archives of Charles Scribner's Sons, Manuscripts Division, Department of Rare Books and Special Collections, Princeton University Library.

26. Review of *Lazy Laughter* by Woodward Boyd, *New York Tribune*, November 22, 1923.

27. Review of *Lazy Laughter* by Woodward Boyd, *Cleveland Plain Dealer*, November 17, 1923.

28. MP to PB, February 7, 1925, the Archives of Charles Scribner's Sons, Manuscripts Division, Department of Rare Books and Special Collections, Princeton University Library.

29. TB to MP, April 14 and 28, 1923, the Archives of Charles Scribner's Sons, Manuscripts Division, Department of Rare Books and Special Collections, Princeton University Library. Published with permission of the Princeton University Library.

30. TB to MP, September 15, 1923, the Archives of Charles Scribner's Sons, Manuscripts Division, Department of Rare Books and Special Collections, Princeton University Library.

31. MP to TB, November 14, 1923, the Archives of Charles Scribner's Sons, Manuscripts Division, Department of Rare Books and Special Collections, Princeton University Library.

32. TB to MP, December 7, 1923, the Archives of Charles Scribner's Sons, Manuscripts Division, Department of Rare Books and Special Collections, Princeton University Library. Published with permission of the Princeton University Library.

33. TB to MP, August 13, 1923, the Archives of Charles Scribner's Sons, Manuscripts Division, Department of Rare Books and Special Collections, Princeton University Library.

34. TB to MP, September 15, 1923, the Archives of Charles Scribner's Sons, Manuscripts Division, Department of Rare Books and Special Collections, Princeton University Library.

35. TB to MP, August 3, 1923, the Archives of Charles Scribner's Sons, Manuscripts Division, Department of Rare Books and Special Collections, Princeton University Library.

36. TB to MP, August 13, 1923, the Archives of Charles Scribner's Sons, Manuscripts Division, Department of Rare Books and Special Collections, Princeton University Library.

37. Elizabeth Grace Boyd, 98–103.

38. TB to ADB, November 23, 1923, Mss 1269 AV, Thomas Boyd Papers, Ohio Historical Society.

39. TB to MP, November 22, 1923, the Archives of Charles Scribner's Sons, Manuscripts Division, Department of Rare Books and Special Collections, Princeton University Library. Published with permission of the Princeton University Library.

40. TB to ADB, November 23, 1923, Mss 1269 AV, Thomas Boyd Papers, Ohio Historical Society.

41. PB to Elinor Merrill, c. November 1923, Mss 1269 AV, Thomas Boyd Papers, Ohio Historical Society.

42. TB to MP, January 4, 1924, the Archives of Charles Scribner's Sons, Manuscripts Division, Department of Rare Books and Special Collections, Princeton University Library.

43. MP to TB, February 9, 1924, the Archives of Charles Scribner's Sons, Manuscripts Division, Department of Rare Books and Special Collections, Princeton University Library.

44. Elizabeth Grace Boyd, 104.

45. Thomas Boyd, *The Dark Cloud* (New York: Charles Scribner's Sons, 1924), 12–13.

46. TB to MP, August 13, 1923, the Archives of Charles Scribner's Sons, Manuscripts Division, Department of Rare Books and Special Collections, Princeton University Library.

47. TB to MP, January 4, 1924, the Archives of Charles Scribner's Sons, Manuscripts Division, Department of Rare Books and Special Collections, Princeton University Library. Published with permission of the Princeton University Library.

48. TB to MP, c. December 7, 1923, the Archives of Charles Scribner's Sons, Manuscripts Division, Department of Rare Books and Special Collections, Princeton University Library.

49. MP to TB, December 7, 1923, the Archives of Charles Scribner's Sons, Manuscripts Division, Department of Rare Books and Special Collections, Princeton University Library. Published with permission of the Princeton University Library.

50. TB to MP, January 4, 1924, the Archives of Charles Scribner's Sons, Manuscripts Division, Department of Rare Books and Special Collections, Princeton University Library. Published with permission of the Princeton University Library.

51. TB to MP, January 16, 1924, the Archives of Charles Scribner's Sons, Manuscripts Division, Department of Rare Books and Special Collections, Princeton University Library. Published with permission of the Princeton University Library.

52. TB to ADB, December 29, 1923, Mss 1269 AV, Thomas Boyd Papers, Ohio Historical Society.

53. TB to Walter Boyd, December 29, 1923, Mss 1269 AV, Thomas Boyd Papers, Ohio Historical Society.

54. TB to MP, January 16, 1924, the Archives of Charles Scribner's Sons, Manuscripts Division, Department of Rare Books and Special Collections, Princeton University Library. Published with permission of the Princeton University Library.

55. TB to ADB, January 29, 1924, Mss 1269 AV, Thomas Boyd Papers, Ohio Historical Society.

56. TB to ADB, January 27, 1924, Mss 1269 AV, Thomas Boyd Papers, Ohio Historical Society.

57. Elizabeth Grace Boyd, 107.

Chapter 5

1. TB to MP, February 27, 1924, and TB to MP, March 2, 1924, the Archives of Charles Scribner's Sons, Manuscripts Division, Department of Rare Books and Special Collections, Princeton University Library. Published with permission of the Princeton University Library.

2. MP to TB, February 9, 1924, the Archives of Charles Scribner's Sons, Manuscripts Division, Department of Rare Books and Special Collections, Princeton University Library.

3. TB to MP, March 2, 1924, the Archives of Charles Scribner's Sons, Manuscripts Division, Department of Rare Books and Special Collections, Princeton University Library. Published with permission of the Princeton University Library.

4. MP to TB, February 21, 1924, the Archives of Charles Scribner's Sons, Manuscripts Division, Department of Rare Books and Special Collections, Princeton University Library.

5. TB to MP, February 27, 1924, the Archives of Charles Scribner's Sons, Manuscripts Division, Department of Rare Books and Special Collections, Princeton University Library.

6. MP to TB, March 1, 1924, the Archives of Charles Scribner's Sons, Manuscripts Division, Department of Rare Books and Special Collections, Princeton University Library.

7. TB to MP, March 2, 1924, the Archives of Charles Scribner's Sons, Manuscripts Division, Department of Rare Books and Special Collections, Princeton University Library. Published with permission of the Princeton University Library.

8. MP to TB, March 6, 1924, the Archives of Charles Scribner's Sons, Manuscripts Division, Department of Rare Books and Special Collections, Princeton University Library.

9. L. E. Pollinger to Charles Scribner's Sons, December 10, 1924, the Archives of Charles Scribner's Sons, Manuscripts Division, Department of Rare Books and Special Collections, Princeton University Library.

10. TB to MP, November 22, 1923, and MP to TB, January 29, 1924, the Archives of Charles Scribner's Sons, Manuscripts Division, Department of Rare Books and Special Collections, Princeton University Library. Published with permission of the Princeton University Library.

11. TB to MP, February 27, 1924, the Archives of Charles Scribner's Sons, Manuscripts Division, Department of Rare Books and Special Collections, Princeton University Library.

12. MP to TB, March 6 and 25, 1924; TB to MP, March 25, 1924; Charles J. Moose to TB, March 25, 1924, the Archives of Charles Scribner's Sons, Manuscripts Division, Department of Rare Books and Special Collections, Princeton University Library.

13. TB to MP, March 5, 1924, the Archives of Charles Scribner's Sons, Manuscripts Division, Department of Rare Books and Special Collections, Princeton University Library.

14. MP to TB, and Robert Bridges to TB, April 1, 1924, the Archives of Charles Scribner's Sons, Manuscripts Division, Department of Rare Books and Special Collections, Princeton University Library.

15. MP to TB, April 30, 1924, the Archives of Charles Scribner's Sons, Manuscripts Division, Department of Rare Books and Special Collections, Princeton University Library.

16. TB to MP, October 27, 1924, the Archives of Charles Scribner's Sons, Manuscripts Division, Department of Rare Books and Special Collections, Princeton University Library.

17. MP to TB, February 9, 1924, and Robert Bridges to PB, March 20, 1924, the Archives of Charles Scribner's Sons, Manuscripts Division, Department of Rare Books and Special Collections, Princeton University Library.

18. TB to MP, May 20 and August 7, 1924, the Archives of Charles Scribner's Sons, Manuscripts Division, Department of Rare Books and Special Collections, Princeton University Library. Published with permission of the Princeton University Library.

19. TB to ADB, March 14, 1924, Mss 1269 AV, Thomas Boyd Papers, Ohio Historical Society.

20. TB to MP, c. March 24, 1924, and MP to TB, March 6, 1924, the Archives of Charles Scribner's Sons, Manuscripts Division, Department of Rare Books and Special Collections, Princeton University Library.

21. TB to ADB, c. March 1924, Mss 1269 AV, Thomas Boyd Papers, Ohio Historical Society.

22. TB to MP, April 28, 1924, the Archives of Charles Scribner's Sons, Manuscripts Division, Department of Rare Books and Special Collections, Princeton University Library. Published with permission of the Princeton University Library.

23. TB to Robert Bridges, March 25, 1924, the Archives of Charles Scribner's Sons, Manuscripts Division, Department of Rare Books and Special Collections, Princeton University Library. Published with permission of the Princeton University Library.

24. MP to TB c. April 1924, Mss 1269 AV, Thomas Boyd Papers, Ohio Historical Society.

25. TB to MP, April 28 and May 20, 1924, the Archives of Charles Scribner's Sons, Manuscripts Division, Department of Rare Books and Special Collections, Princeton University Library. Published with permission of the Princeton University Library.

26. FSF to TB, c. May 1924, Papers of F. Scott Fitzgerald, Manuscripts Division, Department of Rare Books and Special Collections, Princeton University Library. Published with permission of the Princeton University Library.

27. TB to MP, July 2, 1924, the Archives of Charles Scribner's Sons, Manuscripts Division, Department of Rare Books and Special Collections, Princeton University Library. Published with permission of the Princeton University Library.

28. TB to ADB, July 2, 1924, Mss 1269 AV, Thomas Boyd Papers, Ohio Historical Society.

29. Ibid.; TB to MP, July 2, 1924, the Archives of Charles Scribner's Sons, Manuscripts Division, Department of Rare Books and Special Collections, Princeton University Library. Published with permission of the Princeton University Library.

30. TB to ADB, July 2, 1924, Mss 1269 AV, Thomas Boyd Papers, Ohio Historical Society.

31. MP to TB, September 8, 1924, the Archives of Charles Scribner's Sons, Manuscripts Division, Department of Rare Books and Special Collections, Princeton University Library. Published with permission of the Princeton University Library.

32. "Cowards' Courage," review of *The Dark Cloud* by Thomas Boyd, *New York Times Book Review,* September 7, 1924, 8.

33. John Farrar, "Three Novels," review of *The Dark Cloud* by Thomas Boyd, *Bookman* 60 (November 1924): 342.

34. TB to MP, November 11, 1924, the Archives of Charles Scribner's Sons, Manuscripts Division, Department of Rare Books and Special Collections, Princeton University Library. Published with permission of the Princeton University Library.

35. FSF to TB, c. September 1924, Papers of F. Scott Fitzgerald, Manuscripts Division, Department of Rare Books and Special Collections, Princeton University Library. Published with permission of the Princeton University Library.

36. MP to TB, October 20, 1924, the Archives of Charles Scribner's Sons, Manuscripts Division, Department of Rare Books and Special Collections, Princeton University Library.

37. MP to TB, October 31, 1924, the Archives of Charles Scribner's Sons, Manuscripts Division, Department of Rare Books and Special Collections, Princeton University Library.

38. MP to FSF, February 24, 1925, in Kuehl and Bryer, *Dear Scott/Dear Max,* 55–56.

39. TB to MP, c. February 1925, the Archives of Charles Scribner's Sons, Manuscripts Division, Department of Rare Books and Special Collections, Princeton University Library.

40. TB to MP, July 24, 1924, the Archives of Charles Scribner's Sons, Manuscripts Division, Department of Rare Books and Special Collections, Princeton University Library.

41. TB to MP, August 25, 1924, the Archives of Charles Scribner's Sons, Manuscripts Division, Department of Rare Books and Special Collections, Princeton University Library.

42. TB to MP, c. August 30, 1924, the Archives of Charles Scribner's Sons, Manuscripts Division, Department of Rare Books and Special Collections, Princeton University Library.

43. Ibid.; TB to MP, September 28, 1924, the Archives of Charles Scribner's Sons, Manuscripts Division, Department of Rare Books and Special Collections, Princeton University Library.

44. TB to MP, November 15, 1924, the Archives of Charles Scribner's Sons, Manuscripts Division, Department of Rare Books and Special Collections, Princeton University Library.

45. TB to MP, August 7, 1924, the Archives of Charles Scribner's Sons, Manuscripts Division, Department of Rare Books and Special Collections, Princeton University Library. Published with permission of the Princeton University Library.

46. TB to MP, November 11, 1924, the Archives of Charles Scribner's Sons, Manuscripts Division, Department of Rare Books and Special Collections, Princeton University Library. Published with permission of the Princeton University Library.

47. MP to TB, December 2, 1924, the Archives of Charles Scribner's Sons, Manuscripts Division, Department of Rare Books and Special Collections, Princeton University Library. Published with permission of the Princeton University Library.

48. TB to MP, January 6, 1925, the Archives of Charles Scribner's Sons, Manuscripts Division, Department of Rare Books and Special Collections, Princeton University Library.

49. TB to MP, January 15, 1925, the Archives of Charles Scribner's Sons, Manuscripts Division, Department of Rare Books and Special Collections, Princeton University Library.

50. FSF to MP, c. December 20, 1924, in Kuehl and Bryer, *Dear Scott/Dear Max*, 88–91.

51. MP to FSF, February 24, 1925, in Kuehl and Bryer, *Dear Scott/Dear Max*, 94–96.

52. Ibid.; TB to MP, c. February 1925, the Archives of Charles Scribner's Sons, Manuscripts Division, Department of Rare Books and Special Collections, Princeton University Library.

53. TB to MP, c. February 4, 1925, the Archives of Charles Scribner's Sons, Manuscripts Division, Department of Rare Books and Special Collections, Princeton University Library. Published with permission of the Princeton University Library.

54. TB to MP, March 9, 1925, the Archives of Charles Scribner's Sons, Manuscripts Division, Department of Rare Books and Special Collections, Princeton University Library. Published with permission of the Princeton University Library.

55. MP to TB, March 12, 1925, the Archives of Charles Scribner's Sons, Manuscripts Division, Department of Rare Books and Special Collections, Princeton University Library.

56. TB to MP, March 9, 1925, the Archives of Charles Scribner's Sons, Manuscripts Division, Department of Rare Books and Special Collections, Princeton University Library. Published with permission of the Princeton University Library.

57. TB to MP, March 17, 1925, the Archives of Charles Scribner's Sons, Manuscripts Division, Department of Rare Books and Special Collections, Princeton University Library.

58. MP to TB, March 12, 1925, the Archives of Charles Scribner's Sons, Manuscripts Division, Department of Rare Books and Special Collections, Princeton University Library.

59. TB to MP, March 17, 1925, the Archives of Charles Scribner's Sons, Manuscripts Division, Department of Rare Books and Special Collections, Princeton University Library.

60. PB to MP, March 20, 1925, the Archives of Charles Scribner's Sons, Manuscripts Division, Department of Rare Books and Special Collections, Princeton University Library. Published with permission of the Princeton University Library.

61. "Episodes of War," review of *Points of Honor* by Thomas Boyd, *New York Times Book Review*, March 22, 1925, 9, 14.

62. Review of *Points of Honor* by Thomas Boyd, *Nation*, August 20, 1925, 194.

63. FSF to TB, c. June 1925, Papers of F. Scott Fitzgerald, Manuscripts Division, Department of Rare Books and Special Collections, Princeton University Library. Published with permission of the Princeton University Library.

64. FSF to MP, January 31, 1925, in Kuehl and Bryer, *Dear Scott/Dear Max*, 98–99.

65. Thomas Boyd, *Points of Honor* (New York: Scribner's, 1925), viii.

66. MP to TB, March 24, 1925, the Archives of Charles Scribner's Sons, Manuscripts Division, Department of Rare Books and Special Collections, Princeton University Library.

67. MP to TB, March 26, 1925, the Archives of Charles Scribner's Sons, Manuscripts Division, Department of Rare Books and Special Collections, Princeton University Library. Published with permission of the Princeton University Library.

68. MP to FSF, May 9, 1925, in Kuehl and Bryer, *Dear Scott/Dear Max*, 105–6.

69. TB to MP, March 27, 1925, the Archives of Charles Scribner's Sons, Manuscripts Division, Department of Rare Books and Special Collections, Princeton University Library.

70. MP to TB, April 7, 1925, the Archives of Charles Scribner's Sons, Manuscripts Division, Department of Rare Books and Special Collections, Princeton University Library. Published with permission of the Princeton University Library.

71. TB to MP, c. April 10, 1925, the Archives of Charles Scribner's Sons, Manuscripts Division, Department of Rare Books and Special Collections, Princeton University Library. Published with permission of the Princeton University Library.

72. MP to TB, May 16, 1925, the Archives of Charles Scribner's Sons, Manuscripts Division, Department of Rare Books and Special Collections, Princeton University Library.

73. TB to MP, c. April 19, 1925, TB to MP, May 8, 1925, TB to MP, May 18, 1925, the Archives of Charles Scribner's Sons, Manuscripts Division, Department of Rare Books and Special Collections, Princeton University Library.

74. FSF to TB, c. June 1, 1925, F. Scott Fitzgerald Additional Papers, Manuscripts Division, Department of Rare Books and Special Collections, Princeton University Library. Published with permission of the Princeton University Library.

75. Edmund Wilson, ed., *F. Scott Fitzgerald: The Crack Up* (New York: New Directions, 1993), 189–90.

76. FSF to MP, c. June 1, 1925, in *F. Scott Fitzgerald: A Life in Letters*, ed. Matthew J. Bruccoli (New York: Touchstone, 1994), 115–22.

77. FSF to TB, c. June 1, 1925.

78. FSF to MP, February 20, 1926, in Kuehl and Bryer, *Dear Scott/Dear Max*, 133–35.

79. Thomas Boyd, *Samuel Drummond* (New York: Charles Scribner's Sons, 1925), 73.

80. Ibid., 82.

81. TB to MP, July 21, 1925, the Archives of Charles Scribner's Sons, Manuscripts Division, Department of Rare Books and Special Collections, Princeton University Library.

82. Robert Bridges to TB, August 3 and 21, 1925, the Archives of Charles Scribner's Sons, Manuscripts Division, Department of Rare Books and Special Collections, Princeton University Library.

83. TB to MP, c. July 21, 1925, the Archives of Charles Scribner's Sons, Manuscripts Division, Department of Rare Books and Special Collections, Princeton University Library.

84. TB to MP, August 5, 1925, the Archives of Charles Scribner's Sons, Manuscripts Division, Department of Rare Books and Special Collections, Princeton University Library. Published with permission of the Princeton University Library.

85. MP to TB, August 21, 1925, the Archives of Charles Scribner's Sons, Manuscripts Division, Department of Rare Books and Special Collections, Princeton University Library.

86. MP to PB, August 21, 1925, the Archives of Charles Scribner's Sons, Manuscripts Division, Department of Rare Books and Special Collections, Princeton University Library.

87. TB to MP, c. August 1925, the Archives of Charles Scribner's Sons, Manuscripts Division, Department of Rare Books and Special Collections, Princeton University Library.

88. TB to MP, c. August 22, 1925, the Archives of Charles Scribner's Sons, Manuscripts Division, Department of Rare Books and Special Collections, Princeton University Library. Published with permission of the Princeton University Library.

89. "Thomas Boyd, Joins the Rush Back to the Farm," review of *Samuel Drummond* by Thomas Boyd, *New York Times Book Review,* August 30, 1925, 10.

90. John Farrar, "Realism and Fantasy," review of *Samuel Drummond* by Thomas Boyd, *Bookman* 57 (October 1925): 266.

91. MP to TB, October 26, 1925, the Archives of Charles Scribner's Sons, Manuscripts Division, Department of Rare Books and Special Collections, Princeton University Library. Published with permission of the Princeton University Library.

92. TB to MP, December 9, 1925, the Archives of Charles Scribner's Sons, Manuscripts Division, Department of Rare Books and Special Collections, Princeton University Library.

Chapter 6

1. TB to MP, October 20, 1925, the Archives of Charles Scribner's Sons, Manuscripts Division, Department of Rare Books and Special Collections, Princeton University Library. Published with permission of the Princeton University Library.

2. Ibid.

3. Elizabeth Grace Boyd, "Ruth," Mss 1269 AV, Thomas Boyd Papers, Ohio Historical Society.

4. TB to PB, c. December 1925, Mss 1269 AV, Thomas Boyd Papers, Ohio Historical Society.

5. TB to PB (2), c. December 1925, Mss 1269 AV, Thomas Boyd Papers, Ohio Historical Society.

6. TB to PB, c. 1925, Mss 1269 AV, Thomas Boyd Papers, Ohio Historical Society.

7. TB to PB (2), c. 1925, Mss 1269 AV, Thomas Boyd Papers, Ohio Historical Society.

8. TB to MP, c. December 12, 1925, the Archives of Charles Scribner's Sons, Manuscripts Division, Department of Rare Books and Special Collections, Princeton University Library.

9. TB to MP, March 4, 1926, the Archives of Charles Scribner's Sons, Manuscripts Division, Department of Rare Books and Special Collections, Princeton University Library.

10. Robert Bridges to TB, March 18, 1925, the Archives of Charles Scribner's Sons, Manuscripts Division, Department of Rare Books and Special Collections, Princeton University Library.

11. TB to Robert Bridges, c. August 1926, the Archives of Charles Scribner's Sons, Manuscripts Division, Department of Rare Books and Special Collections, Princeton University Library. Published with permission of the Princeton University Library.

12. TB to MP, c. December 22, 1925, the Archives of Charles Scribner's Sons, Manuscripts Division, Department of Rare Books and Special Collections, Princeton University Library.

13. TB to MP, c. March 25, 1926, the Archives of Charles Scribner's Sons, Manuscripts Division, Department of Rare Books and Special Collections, Princeton University Library.

14. TB to MP, June 30, 1926, the Archives of Charles Scribner's Sons, Manuscripts Division, Department of Rare Books and Special Collections, Princeton University Library.

15. TB to MP, August 17, 1926, the Archives of Charles Scribner's Sons, Manuscripts Division, Department of Rare Books and Special Collections, Princeton University Library. Published with permission of the Princeton University Library.

16. MP to FSF, November 4, 1926, in Kuehl and Bryer, *Dear Scott/Dear Max*, 143–44.

17. FSF to MP, May 8, 1926, in Kuehl and Bryer, *Dear Scott/Dear Max*, 140–41.

18. MP to FSF, November 4, 1926, in Kuehl and Bryer, *Dear Scott/Dear Max*, 143–44.

19. TB to MP, March 24, 1927, the Archives of Charles Scribner's Sons, Manuscripts Division, Department of Rare Books and Special Collections, Princeton University Library.

20. MP to PB, February 8, 1926, the Archives of Charles Scribner's Sons, Manuscripts Division, Department of Rare Books and Special Collections, Princeton University Library.

21. MP to PB, July 14, 1927, the Archives of Charles Scribner's Sons, Manuscripts Division, Department of Rare Books and Special Collections, Princeton University Library.

22. MP to TB, May 10, 1927, the Archives of Charles Scribner's Sons, Manuscripts Division, Department of Rare Books and Special Collections, Princeton University Library. Published with permission of the Princeton University Library.

23. Ibid.

24. TB to MP, c. June 3, 1927, the Archives of Charles Scribner's Sons, Manuscripts Division, Department of Rare Books and Special Collections, Princeton University Library. Published with permission of the Princeton University Library.

25. MP to TB, June 3, 1927, the Archives of Charles Scribner's Sons, Manuscripts Division, Department of Rare Books and Special Collections, Princeton University Library.

26. TB to MP, March 24, 1927, the Archives of Charles Scribner's Sons, Manuscripts Division, Department of Rare Books and Special Collections, Princeton University Library.

27. TB to MP, c. December 9, 1927, the Archives of Charles Scribner's Sons, Manuscripts Division, Department of Rare Books and Special Collections, Princeton University Library. Published with permission of the Princeton University Library.

28. MP to TB, December 9, 1927, the Archives of Charles Scribner's Sons, Manuscripts Division, Department of Rare Books and Special Collections, Princeton University Library.

29. Thomas Boyd, *Simon Girty: The White Savage* (New York: Minton Balch & Company, 1928), 63–64.

30. TB to MP, c. September 1927, the Archives of Charles Scribner's Sons, Manuscripts Division, Department of Rare Books and Special Collections, Princeton University Library.

31. MP to TB, October 14, 1927, the Archives of Charles Scribner's Sons, Manuscripts Division, Department of Rare Books and Special Collections, Princeton University Library.

32. MP to TB, October 21, 1927, the Archives of Charles Scribner's Sons, Manuscripts Division, Department of Rare Books and Special Collections, Princeton University Library.

33. TB to MP, c. October 21, 1927, the Archives of Charles Scribner's Sons, Manuscripts Division, Department of Rare Books and Special Collections, Princeton University Library. Published with permission of the Princeton University Library.

34. MP to TB, October 28, 1927, the Archives of Charles Scribner's Sons, Manuscripts Division, Department of Rare Books and Special Collections, Princeton University Library.

35. TB to MP, c. November 2, 1927, the Archives of Charles Scribner's Sons, Manuscripts Division, Department of Rare Books and Special Collections, Princeton University Library.

36. MP to TB, December 1, 1927, the Archives of Charles Scribner's Sons, Manuscripts Division, Department of Rare Books and Special Collections, Princeton University Library.

37. TB to MP, c. November 1927, the Archives of Charles Scribner's Sons, Manuscripts Division, Department of Rare Books and Special Collections, Princeton University Library.

38. TB to MP, January 3, 1928, the Archives of Charles Scribner's Sons, Manuscripts Division, Department of Rare Books and Special Collections, Princeton University Library.

39. TB to MP, January 12, 1928; MP to TB, January 23, 1928, the Archives of Charles Scribner's Sons, Manuscripts Division, Department of Rare Books and Special Collections, Princeton University Library.

40. TB to MP, January 27, 1928, the Archives of Charles Scribner's Sons, Manuscripts Division, Department of Rare Books and Special Collections, Princeton University Library.

41. Elizabeth Grace Boyd, "Ruth," Mss 1269 AV, Thomas Boyd Papers, Ohio Historical Society.

42. Berg, *Max Perkins*, 225.

43. TB to MP, c. February 24, 1928, the Archives of Charles Scribner's Sons, Manuscripts Division, Department of Rare Books and Special Collections, Princeton University Library. Published with permission of the Princeton University Library.

44. MP to TB, February 24, 1928, the Archives of Charles Scribner's Sons, Manuscripts Division, Department of Rare Books and Special Collections, Princeton University Library.

45. TB to MP, c. February 24, 1928, the Archives of Charles Scribner's Sons, Manuscripts Division, Department of Rare Books and Special Collections, Princeton University Library. Published with permission of the Princeton University Library.

46. TB to PB, c. February 1928, Mss 1269 AV, Thomas Boyd Papers, Ohio Historical Society.

47. PB to TB, March 3, 1928, Mss 1269 AV, Thomas Boyd Papers, Ohio Historical Society.

48. TB to MP, March 23, 1928, the Archives of Charles Scribner's Sons, Manuscripts Division, Department of Rare Books and Special Collections, Princeton University Library.

49. MP to TB, February 10, 1928, the Archives of Charles Scribner's Sons, Manuscripts Division, Department of Rare Books and Special Collections, Princeton University Library.

50. MP to TB, April 28, 1928, the Archives of Charles Scribner's Sons, Manuscripts Division, Department of Rare Books and Special Collections, Princeton University Library.

51. Thomas Boyd, *Shadow of the Long Knives* (New York: Charles Scribner's Sons, 1928), 336.

52. "The Colonial Frontier in a New Novel by Thomas Boyd," review of *Shadow of the Long Knives* by Thomas Boyd, *New York Times Book Review*, June 10, 1928, 8.

53. Review of *Shadow of the Long Knives* by Thomas Boyd, *Providence Journal Sunday Magazine*, June 3, 1928, 26.

54. MP to TB, June 4, 1928, the Archives of Charles Scribner's Sons, Manuscripts Division, Department of Rare Books and Special Collections, Princeton University Library. Published with permission of the Princeton University Library.

55. MP to TB, June 14 and November 28, 1928, the Archives of Charles Scribner's Sons, Manuscripts Division, Department of Rare Books and Special Collections, Princeton University Library.

56. MP to TB, May 26, 1928, the Archives of Charles Scribner's Sons, Manuscripts Division, Department of Rare Books and Special Collections, Princeton University Library. Published with permission of the Princeton University Library.

57. TB to MP, June 10, 1928, the Archives of Charles Scribner's Sons, Manuscripts Division, Department of Rare Books and Special Collections, Princeton University Library. Published with permission of the Princeton University Library.

58. TB to MP, c. June 26, 1928, the Archives of Charles Scribner's Sons, Manuscripts Division, Department of Rare Books and Special Collections, Princeton University Library. Published with permission of the Princeton University Library.

59. MP to TB, June 26, 1928, the Archives of Charles Scribner's Sons, Manuscripts Division, Department of Rare Books and Special Collections, Princeton University Library. Published with permission of the Princeton University Library.

60. TB to MP, June 20, 1928, the Archives of Charles Scribner's Sons, Manuscripts Division, Department of Rare Books and Special Collections, Princeton University Library.

61. MP to TB, August 6 and 17, 1928, the Archives of Charles Scribner's Sons, Manuscripts Division, Department of Rare Books and Special Collections, Princeton University Library.

62. TB to MP, August 17, 1928, the Archives of Charles Scribner's Sons, Manuscripts Division, Department of Rare Books and Special Collections, Princeton University Library. Published with permission of the Princeton University Library.

63. MP to TB, August 28, 1928, the Archives of Charles Scribner's Sons, Manuscripts Division, Department of Rare Books and Special Collections, Princeton University Library.

64. TB to MP, c. September 15, 1928, the Archives of Charles Scribner's Sons, Manuscripts Division, Department of Rare Books and Special Collections, Princeton University Library.

65. TB to MP, c. October 1928, the Archives of Charles Scribner's Sons, Manuscripts Division, Department of Rare Books and Special Collections, Princeton University Library.

66. TB to MP, November 6 and December 1, 1928, the Archives of Charles Scribner's Sons, Manuscripts Division, Department of Rare Books and Special Collections, Princeton University Library.

67. Robert Bridges to TB, December 7, 1928, the Archives of Charles Scribner's Sons, Manuscripts Division, Department of Rare Books and Special Collections, Princeton University Library.

68. MP to TB, January 2, 1929, the Archives of Charles Scribner's Sons, Manu-

scripts Division, Department of Rare Books and Special Collections, Princeton University Library. Published with permission of the Princeton University Library.

69. TB to MP, January 23, 1929, the Archives of Charles Scribner's Sons, Manuscripts Division, Department of Rare Books and Special Collections, Princeton University Library. Published with permission of the Princeton University Library.

70. Margaret Shane to Granville Hicks, November 25, 1941, Papers of Granville Hicks, Department of Special Collections, Syracuse University Libraries.

71. TB to ADB, 1928 or 1929, Mss 1269 AV, Thomas Boyd Papers, Ohio Historical Society.

72. Margaret Shane to Granville Hicks, November 25, 1941, Papers of Granville Hicks, Department of Special Collections, Syracuse University Libraries.

73. TB to MP, c. April 16, 1929, the Archives of Charles Scribner's Sons, Manuscripts Division, Department of Rare Books and Special Collections, Princeton University Library.

74. TB to MP, c. June 18, 1929, the Archives of Charles Scribner's Sons, Manuscripts Division, Department of Rare Books and Special Collections, Princeton University Library.

75. Tax return of Thomas Boyd for the year 1928, Mss 1269 AV, Thomas Boyd Papers, Ohio Historical Society.

76. Bank statement of Thomas Boyd for April 1929, Mss 1269 AV, Thomas Boyd Papers, Ohio Historical Society.

77. TB to MP, February 22, 1929, the Archives of Charles Scribner's Sons, Manuscripts Division, Department of Rare Books and Special Collections, Princeton University Library.

78. TB to MP, c. May 1929, the Archives of Charles Scribner's Sons, Manuscripts Division, Department of Rare Books and Special Collections, Princeton University Library. Published with permission of the Princeton University Library.

79. TB to MP, c. April 16, 1929, the Archives of Charles Scribner's Sons, Manuscripts Division, Department of Rare Books and Special Collections, Princeton University Library.

80. MP to TB, April 16, 1929, the Archives of Charles Scribner's Sons, Manuscripts Division, Department of Rare Books and Special Collections, Princeton University Library.

81. TB to MP, c. April 23, 1929, the Archives of Charles Scribner's Sons, Manuscripts Division, Department of Rare Books and Special Collections, Princeton University Library.

82. MP to TB, April 23, 1929, the Archives of Charles Scribner's Sons, Manuscripts Division, Department of Rare Books and Special Collections, Princeton University Library.

83. TB to MP, April 25, 1929, the Archives of Charles Scribner's Sons, Manuscripts

Division, Department of Rare Books and Special Collections, Princeton University Library.

84. TB to MP, c. April 29, 1929, the Archives of Charles Scribner's Sons, Manuscripts Division, Department of Rare Books and Special Collections, Princeton University Library.

85. MP to TB, May 31, 1929, the Archives of Charles Scribner's Sons, Manuscripts Division, Department of Rare Books and Special Collections, Princeton University Library. Published with permission of the Princeton University Library. Contract issued for a biography of Alexander Hamilton to Thomas Boyd, Mss 1269 AV, Thomas Boyd Papers, Ohio Historical Society.

86. TB to MP, c. June 24, 1929, the Archives of Charles Scribner's Sons, Manuscripts Division, Department of Rare Books and Special Collections, Princeton University Library.

87. Lella Northington to Wallace Meyer, July 29, 1929, Mss 1269 AV, Thomas Boyd Papers, Ohio Historical Society.

88. Elizabeth Grace Boyd, "Ruth," Mss 1269 AV, Thomas Boyd Papers, Ohio Historical Society.

89. TB to MP, August 8, 1929, the Archives of Charles Scribner's Sons, Manuscripts Division, Department of Rare Books and Special Collections, Princeton University Library.

90. Thomas Boyd, "Extreme Mental Cruelty," *Ladies' Home Journal*, March 1930, 12.

Chapter 7

1. Elizabeth Grace Boyd, "Ruth," Mss 1269 AV, Thomas Boyd Papers, Ohio Historical Society. Elizabeth Grace Nash, Cocoa Beach, Florida, to Brian Bruce, Pearland, Texas, April 4, 1996.

2. TB to MP, August 8 and September 8, 1929, the Archive of Charles Scribner's Sons, Manuscripts Division, Department of Rare Books and Special Collections, Princeton University Library.

3. Thatcher and Woodburn to PB, November 12, 1929, Mss 1269 AV, Thomas Boyd Papers, Ohio Historical Society.

4. TB to PB, c. 1930, Mss 1269 AV, Thomas Boyd Papers, Ohio Historical Society.

5. Ibid.

6. TB to PB, March 10, 1930, Mss 1269 AV, Thomas Boyd Papers, Ohio Historical Society.

7. Elizabeth Grace Boyd, "Ruth," Mss 1269 AV, Thomas Boyd Papers, Ohio Historical Society.

8. TB to MP, November 24, 1929, the Archives of Charles Scribner's Sons, Manuscripts Division, Department of Rare Books and Special Collections, Princeton University Library.

9. Review of *Mad Anthony Wayne* by Thomas Boyd, *Bookman* 70 (January 1930): 564–65.

10. Review of *Mad Anthony Wayne* by Thomas Boyd, *New York Herald Tribune*, October 29, 1929.

11. MP to TB, November 18, 1929, and February 10, 1930, the Archives of Charles Scribner's Sons, Manuscripts Division, Department of Rare Books and Special Collections, Princeton University Library.

12. Elizabeth Grace Boyd, "Ruth," Mss 1269 AV, Thomas Boyd Papers, Ohio Historical Society.

13. TB to MP, February 12, 1930, the Archives of Charles Scribner's Sons, Manuscripts Division, Department of Rare Books and Special Collections, Princeton University Library.

14. TB to MP, March 18, 1930, the Archives of Charles Scribner's Sons, Manuscripts Division, Department of Rare Books and Special Collections, Princeton University Library. Published with permission of the Princeton University Library.

15. TB to MP, April 7 and 27, 1930, the Archives of Charles Scribner's Sons, Manuscripts Division, Department of Rare Books and Special Collections, Princeton University Library.

16. TB to MP, May 15, 1930, the Archives of Charles Scribner's Sons, Manuscripts Division, Department of Rare Books and Special Collections, Princeton University Library.

17. TB to MP, June 10, 1930, the Archives of Charles Scribner's Sons, Manuscripts Division, Department of Rare Books and Special Collections, Princeton University Library.

18. TB to MP, August 15, 1930, the Archives of Charles Scribner's Sons, Manuscripts Division, Department of Rare Books and Special Collections, Princeton University Library.

19. TB to MP, c. October 18, 1930, the Archives of Charles Scribner's Sons, Manuscripts Division, Department of Rare Books and Special Collections, Princeton University Library.

20. MP to TB, October 18, 1930, the Archives of Charles Scribner's Sons, Manuscripts Division, Department of Rare Books and Special Collections, Princeton University Library.

21. TB to MP, March 18, 1930, the Archives of Charles Scribner's Sons, Manuscripts Division, Department of Rare Books and Special Collections, Princeton University Library. Published with permission of the Princeton University Library.

22. TB to MP, June 18, 1930, the Archives of Charles Scribner's Sons, Manuscripts Division, Department of Rare Books and Special Collections, Princeton University Library. Published with permission of the Princeton University Library.

23. MP to TB, June 20, 1930, the Archives of Charles Scribner's Sons, Manuscripts Division, Department of Rare Books and Special Collections, Princeton University Library. Published with permission of the Princeton University Library.

24. TB to MP, c. July 9, 1930, the Archives of Charles Scribner's Sons, Manuscripts Division, Department of Rare Books and Special Collections, Princeton University Library.

25. MP to TB, September 19, 1930, the Archives of Charles Scribner's Sons, Manuscripts Division, Department of Rare Books and Special Collections, Princeton University Library.

26. TB to MP, c. September 22, 1930, the Archives of Charles Scribner's Sons, Manuscripts Division, Department of Rare Books and Special Collections, Princeton University Library. Published with permission of the Princeton University Library.

27. TB to MP, c. October 18, 1930, the Archives of Charles Scribner's Sons, Manuscripts Division, Department of Rare Books and Special Collections, Princeton University Library.

28. Alfred Dashiell to TB, November 5, 1930, the Archives of Charles Scribner's Sons, Manuscripts Division, Department of Rare Books and Special Collections, Princeton University Library. Published with permission of the Princeton University Library.

29. TB to MP, c. November 5, 1930, the Archives of Charles Scribner's Sons, Manuscripts Division, Department of Rare Books and Special Collections, Princeton University Library. Published with permission of the Princeton University Library.

30. TB to MP, November 23, 1930, the Archives of Charles Scribner's Sons, Manuscripts Division, Department of Rare Books and Special Collections, Princeton University Library.

31. TB to MP, November 25, 1930, the Archives of Charles Scribner's Sons, Manuscripts Division, Department of Rare Books and Special Collections, Princeton University Library.

32. MP to TB, November 29, 1930, the Archives of Charles Scribner's Sons, Manuscripts Division, Department of Rare Books and Special Collections, Princeton University Library.

33. TB to MP, c. December 3, 1930, the Archives of Charles Scribner's Sons, Manuscripts Division, Department of Rare Books and Special Collections, Princeton University Library.

34. TB to MP, December 14, 1930, the Archives of Charles Scribner's Sons, Manuscripts Division, Department of Rare Books and Special Collections, Princeton University Library.

35. MP to TB, January 4, 1931, the Archives of Charles Scribner's Sons, Manuscripts Division, Department of Rare Books and Special Collections, Princeton University Library. Published with permission of the Princeton University Library.

36. Elizabeth Grace Boyd, "Ruth," Mss 1269 AV, Thomas Boyd Papers, Ohio Historical Society.

37. TB to RFB, c. January–February 1931, Ruth Fitch Mason Papers, Department of Special Collections, Vassar College Libraries.

38. TB to RFB, c. January–February 1931 (2), Ruth Fitch Mason Papers, Department of Special Collections, Vassar College Libraries.

39. TB to RFB, c. March 1931, Ruth Fitch Mason Papers, Department of Special Collections, Vassar College Libraries.

40. TB to RFB, 2 letters c. March 1931, Ruth Fitch Mason Papers, Department of Special Collections, Vassar College Libraries.

41. TB to RFB, March 20, 1931, Ruth Fitch Mason Papers, Department of Special Collections, Vassar College Libraries.

42. TB to RFB, March 14, 1931, Ruth Fitch Mason Papers, Department of Special Collections, Vassar College Libraries.

43. TB to RFB, March 17, 1931, Ruth Fitch Mason Papers, Department of Special Collections, Vassar College Libraries.

44. TB to RFB, c. March 24, 1931, Ruth Fitch Mason Papers, Department of Special Collections, Vassar College Libraries.

45. TB to RFB, March 24, 1931, Ruth Fitch Mason Papers, Department of Special Collections, Vassar College Libraries.

46. TB to RFB, March 20, 1931, Ruth Fitch Mason Papers, Department of Special Collections, Vassar College Libraries.

47. TB to RFB, c. March 20, 1931, Ruth Fitch Mason Papers, Department of Special Collections, Vassar College Libraries.

48. Louise Mansfield Field, review of *Light Horse Harry Lee*, by Thomas Boyd, *Bookman* 73 (May 1931): 303.

49. MP to TB, April 30, 1931, the Archives of Charles Scribner's Sons, Manuscripts Division, Department of Rare Books and Special Collections, Princeton University Library.

50. Ibid. MP to RFB, June 6, 1936, the Archives of Charles Scribner's Sons, Manuscripts Division, Department of Rare Books and Special Collections, Princeton University Library.

51. TB to PB, c. March 1931, The Personal Collection of Brainerd F. Phillipson.

52. TB to PB (2), c. March 1931, Mss 1269 AV, Thomas Boyd Papers, Ohio Historical Society.

53. Betty Grace Nash, Cocoa Beach, Florida, to Brian Bruce, Pearland, Texas, April 4, 1996.

54. TB to RFB, c. March 1931, Mss 1269 AV, Thomas Boyd Papers, Ohio Historical Society.

55. TB to RFB, c. March 1931, Ruth Fitch Mason Papers, Department of Special Collections, Vassar College Libraries. TB to PB, 2 letters, c. 1931, Mss 1269 AV, Thomas Boyd Papers, Ohio Historical Society.

56. TB to RFB, c. March 20, 1931, Ruth Fitch Mason Papers, Department of Special Collections, Vassar College Libraries.

57. TB to RFB, c. March 1931, Ruth Fitch Mason Papers, Department of Special Collections, Vassar College Libraries.

58. TB to Peggy Boyd Shane, c. April 1931, Mss 1269 AV, Thomas Boyd Papers, Ohio Historical Society.

59. Elizabeth Grace Boyd, "Ruth," Mss 1269 AV, Thomas Boyd Papers, Ohio Historical Society.

60. TB to MP, c. April 3, 1931, the Archives of Charles Scribner's Sons, Manuscripts Division, Department of Rare Books and Special Collections, Princeton University Library.

61. TB to MP, c. April 20, 1931, the Archives of Charles Scribner's Sons, Manuscripts Division, Department of Rare Books and Special Collections, Princeton University Library.

62. TB to MP, c. May 25, 1931, the Archives of Charles Scribner's Sons, Manuscripts Division, Department of Rare Books and Special Collections, Princeton University Library.

63. TB to MP, c. August 31, 1931, the Archives of Charles Scribner's Sons, Manuscripts Division, Department of Rare Books and Special Collections, Princeton University Library.

64. TB to Peggy Boyd Shane, c. July 1931, Mss 1269 AV, Thomas Boyd Papers, Ohio Historical Society.

65. TB to Peggy Boyd Shane, c. August 1931, Mss 1269 AV, Thomas Boyd Papers, Ohio Historical Society.

66. Ibid. TB to EGB, c. August 1931, Mss 1269 AV, Thomas Boyd Papers, Ohio Historical Society.

67. FSF to MP, c. 1930, in *F. Scott Fitzgerald: A Life in Letters*, ed. Matthew J. Bruccoli (New York: Touchstone, 1994), 174.

68. Elizabeth Grace Boyd, "Ruth," Mss 1269 AV, Thomas Boyd Papers, Ohio Historical Society.

69. TB to Peggy Boyd Shane, c. August 1931, Mss 1269 AV, Thomas Boyd Papers, Ohio Historical Society.

70. TB to MP, August 31, 1931, the Archives of Charles Scribner's Sons, Manuscripts Division, Department of Rare Books and Special Collections, Princeton University Library.

71. TB to MP, c. September 24, 1931, the Archives of Charles Scribner's Sons, Manuscripts Division, Department of Rare Books and Special Collections, Princeton University Library.

72. MP to TB, September 24, 1931, and TB to MP, c. September 24, 1924, the Archives of Charles Scribner's Sons, Manuscripts Division, Department of Rare Books and Special Collections, Princeton University Library.

73. TB to MP, October 16, 1931, the Archives of Charles Scribner's Sons, Manuscripts Division, Department of Rare Books and Special Collections, Princeton University Library.

74. Alfred Dashiell to Carl Brandt, November 6, 1931, the Archives of Charles Scribner's Sons, Manuscripts Division, Department of Rare Books and Special Collections, Princeton University Library. Published with permission of the Princeton University Library.

75. MP to TB, November 12, 1931, the Archives of Charles Scribner's Sons, Manuscripts Division, Department of Rare Books and Special Collections, Princeton University Library.

76. TB to MP, c. November 18, 1931, the Archives of Charles Scribner's Sons, Manuscripts Division, Department of Rare Books and Special Collections, Princeton University Library. Published with permission of the Princeton University Library.

77. MP to TB, November 18, 1931, the Archives of Charles Scribner's Sons, Manuscripts Division, Department of Rare Books and Special Collections, Princeton University Library.

Chapter 8

1. TB to Peggy Boyd Shane, c. May 1932, Mss 1269 AV, Thomas Boyd Papers, Ohio Historical Society.

2. Mary Grace Canfield, *The Valley of the Kedron* (South Woodstock, Vt.: Kedron Associates, 1940), 94.

3. TB to Peggy Boyd Shane, c. September 1932, Mss 1269 AV, Thomas Boyd Papers, Ohio Historical Society.

4. TB to MP, March 21, 1932, the Archives of Charles Scribner's Sons, Manuscripts Division, Department of Rare Books and Special Collections, Princeton University Library. Published with permission of the Princeton University Library.

5. TB to MP, August 25, 1932, the Archives of Charles Scribner's Sons, Manuscripts Division, Department of Rare Books and Special Collections, Princeton University Library.

6. MP to TB, October 10, 1932, the Archives of Charles Scribner's Sons, Manuscripts Division, Department of Rare Books and Special Collections, Princeton University Library.

7. MP to TB, August 30, 1932, the Archives of Charles Scribner's Sons, Manuscripts Division, Department of Rare Books and Special Collections, Princeton University Library.

8. TB to MP, c. December 12, 1932, the Archives of Charles Scribner's Sons, Manuscripts Division, Department of Rare Books and Special Collections, Princeton University Library. Published with permission of the Princeton University Library.

9. Ibid.

10. TB to MP, c. March 21, 1933, the Archives of Charles Scribner's Sons, Manuscripts Division, Department of Rare Books and Special Collections, Princeton University Library.

11. TB to Peggy Boyd Shane, 2 letters, 1933 or 1934, Mss 1269 AV, Thomas Boyd Papers, Ohio Historical Society.

12. TB to MP, March 31, 1933, the Archives of Charles Scribner's Sons, Manuscripts Division, Department of Rare Books and Special Collections, Princeton University Library.

13. MP to TB, March 21, 1933, the Archives of Charles Scribner's Sons, Manuscripts Division, Department of Rare Books and Special Collections, Princeton University Library.

14. TB to Peggy Boyd Shane, c. March 1933, Mss 1269 AV, Thomas Boyd Papers, Ohio Historical Society.

15. TB to MP, c. April 3, 1934, the Archives of Charles Scribner's Sons, Manuscripts Division, Department of Rare Books and Special Collections, Princeton University Library.

16. TB to MP, April 25, 1934, the Archives of Charles Scribner's Sons, Manuscripts Division, Department of Rare Books and Special Collections, Princeton University Library.

17. MP to TB, May 17, 1934, the Archives of Charles Scribner's Sons, Manuscripts Division, Department of Rare Books and Special Collections, Princeton University Library.

18. TB to MP, c. August 28, 1934, the Archives of Charles Scribner's Sons, Manuscripts Division, Department of Rare Books and Special Collections, Princeton University Library. Published with permission of the Princeton University Library.

19. TB to ADB, c. 1932, Mss 1269 AV, Thomas Boyd Papers, Ohio Historical Society.

20. TB to Peggy Boyd Shane, c. 1933, Mss 1269 AV, Thomas Boyd Papers, Ohio Historical Society.

21. RFB to Granville Hicks, November 30, 1941, Papers of Granville Hicks, Syracuse University Libraries.

22. Elizabeth Grace Boyd, "Ruth," Mss 1269 AV, Thomas Boyd Papers, Ohio Historical Society.

23. Ibid.

24. Granville Hicks to EGB, March 15, 1943, Mss 1269 AV, Thomas Boyd Papers, Ohio Historical Society.

25. Communist Party campaign pamphlet, Massachusetts Communist Party, 1934, Mss 1269 AV, Thomas Boyd Papers, Ohio Historical Society.

26. Boyd, *In Time of Peace*, 309.

27. Review of *In Time of Peace* by Thomas Boyd, *Nation* 22 (May 1935): 609.

28. Granville Hicks, "Thomas Boyd, Communist," in *Granville Hicks in the New Masses*, ed. Jack Alan Robbins (Port Washington, New York: Kennikar Press, 1974), 325.

29. Mary Reed to Pat Toohey, September 6, 1938, in *The Soviet World of American Communism* by Harvey Klehr, John Earl Haynes, and Kyrill M. Anderson (New Haven: Yale University Press, 1998), 342.

30. Pat Toohey to Mary Reed, c. September 6, 1938, in Klehr, Haynes, and Anderson, *The Soviet World of American Communism*, 343.

31. Thomas Boyd, *Poor John Fitch, Inventor of the Steamboat* (New York: Putnam, 1935), 194.

32. TB to Peggy Boyd Shane, c. 1934, Mss 1269 AV, Thomas Boyd Papers, Ohio Historical Society.

33. "Thomas Boyd," obituary, *New York Times*, January 27, 1935.

34. TB to Peggy Boyd Shane, January 26, 1935, Mss 1269 AV, Thomas Boyd Papers, Ohio Historical Society.

35. Duncan Smith to Peggy Boyd Shane, January 27, 1935, Mss 1269 AV, Thomas Boyd Papers, Ohio Historical Society.

36. Duncan Smith to Peggy Boyd Shane, January 28, 1935, Mss 1269 AV, Thomas Boyd Papers, Ohio Historical Society.

37. "Thomas Boyd," obituary, *New York Times*.

38. The Board of Veterans Appeals, Boyd, Thomas A., XC-507, 735, August 31, 1939, pp. 1–4, Mss 1269 AV, Thomas Boyd Papers, Ohio Historical Society.

39. Elizabeth Boyd Nash, Cocoa Beach, Florida, to Brian Bruce, Pearland, Texas, April 4, 1996.

Bibliography

Primary Sources

Collections

Much of this work is based on information found in letters and other documents located in one of the following collections:

Archives of Charles Scribner's Sons, Manuscripts Division, Department of Rare Books and Special Collections, Princeton University Library.

F. Scott Fitzgerald Additional Papers, Manuscripts Division, Department of Rare Books and Special Collections, Princeton University Library.

F. Scott Fitzgerald Papers, Manuscripts Division, Department of Rare Books and Special Collections, Princeton University Library.

Papers of Granville Hicks, Syracuse University Libraries.

The Personal Collection of Brainerd F. Phillipson, Holliston, Mass.

The Ruth Fitch Mason Papers, Department of Special Collections, Vassar College Libraries.

The Thomas Boyd Papers, The Ohio Historical Society.

Books by Thomas Boyd

In Time of Peace. New York: Minton Balch and Company, 1935.

Points of Honor. New York: Charles Scribner's Sons, 1925.

Poor John Fitch, Inventor of the Steamboat. New York: Minton Balch Putnam, 1935.

Samuel Drummond. New York: Charles Scribner's Sons, 1925.

Shadow of the Long Knives. New York: Charles Scribner's Sons, 1928.

Simon Girty: The White Savage. New York: Minton Balch and Company, 1928.

The Dark Cloud. New York: Charles Scribner's Sons, 1924.

Through the Wheat. New York: Charles Scribner's Sons, 1923.

Stories and Reviews by Thomas Boyd

"Extreme Mental Cruelty." *Ladies' Home Journal* 9 (March 1930): 12, 114–22.

In a Corner with the Bookworm. *St. Paul Daily News*, City Life section: March 20, 26, 1921; February 26, 1922; September 17, 1922.

"Literary Libels: Carl Sandburg." In a Corner with the Bookworm, *St. Paul Daily News*, April 9, 1922, City Life section, p. 6.

"Literary Libels: F. Scott Fitzgerald." In a Corner with the Bookworm, *St. Paul Daily News*, March 5, 12, 17, 1922, City Life section, p. 6.

"The Long Shot," story in *Points of Honor* by Thomas Boyd. New York: Charles Scribner's Sons, 1925.

"A Mental Vivisectionist." In a Corner with the Bookworm, *St. Paul Daily News*, October 8, 1922, City Life section, p. 6.

"Sinclair Lewis' Last Novel." In a Corner with the Bookworm, *St. Paul Daily News*, September 17, 1922, City Life section, p. 6.

Articles and Reviews

"Cowards' Courage," review of *The Dark Cloud* by Thomas Boyd. *New York Times Book Review*, September 7, 1924, 8.

Crawford, John W. "A Malicious Panorama," review of *Through the Wheat* by Thomas Boyd. *Nation* 117 (May 1923): 66.

"Episodes of War," review of *Points of Honor* by Thomas Boyd. *New York Times Book Review*, March 22, 1925, 9, 14.

Farrar, John. "Realism and Fantasy," review of *Samuel Drummond* by Thomas Boyd. *Bookman* 57 (October 1925): 266.

———. "Three Novels," review of *The Dark Cloud* by Thomas Boyd. *Bookman* 60 (November 1924): 342.

Field, Louise Mansfield. Review of *Light Horse Harry Lee* by Thomas Boyd. *Bookman* 73 (May 1931): 303.

Fitzgerald, F. Scott. "A Rugged Novel," review of *The Love Legend* by Woodward Boyd. *Literary Review: New York Evening Post*, October 28, 1922, 143.

———. "Under Fire," review of *Through the Wheat* by Thomas Boyd. *Literary Review: New York Evening Post*, May 26, 1923, 715.

Hicks, Granville. "Thomas Boyd, Communist." In *Granville Hicks in the New Masses*, ed. Jack Alan Robbins, 323–27. Port Washington, N.Y.: Kennikar Press, 1974.

"Latest Works of Fiction," review of *Through the Wheat* by Thomas Boyd. *New York Times Book Review*, April 29, 1923, 14.

Review of *In Time of Peace* by Thomas Boyd. *Nation* 22 (May 1935): 609.

Review of *Lazy Laughter* by Woodward Boyd. *New York Tribune*, November 22, 1923.

Review of *Lazy Laughter* by Woodward Boyd. *Cleveland Plain Dealer*, November 17, 1923.

Review of *The Love Legend* by Woodward Boyd. *Chicago Daily News*, November 8, 1922.
Review of *Mad Anthony Wayne* by Thomas Boyd. *Bookman* 70 (January 1930): 564–65.
Review of *Mad Anthony Wayne* by Thomas Boyd. *New York Herald Tribune*, October 29, 1929.
Review of *Shadow of the Long Knives* by Thomas Boyd. *Providence Journal Sunday Magazine*, June 3, 1928, 26.
"The Colonial Frontier in a New Novel by Thomas Boyd," review of *Shadow of the Long Knives* by Thomas Boyd. *New York Times Book Review*, June 10, 1928, 8.
"Thomas Boyd Joins the Rush Back to the Farm," review of *Samuel Drummond* by Thomas Boyd. *New York Times Book Review*, August 30, 1925, 10.
"Thomas Boyd," obituary. *New York Times*, January 27, 1925, 1.
Wilson, Edmund. Review of *Through the Wheat* by Thomas Boyd. *Dial* (July 1923): 93–95.
"Woodward Boyd's *The Love Legend*," review of *The Love Legend* by Woodward Boyd. *New York Times Book Review*, October 28, 1922, 14.

Secondary Sources

Berg, A. Scott. *Max Perkins: Editor of Genius*. New York: Riverhead Books/ The Berkley Publishing Group, 1978.
Boyd, Elizabeth Grace. "Ruth." Unpublished manuscript. The Personal Collection of Brainerd F. Phillipson, Holliston, Mass.
———. Untitled biography of Thomas Boyd. Senior Thesis, Vassar College, 1943.
Bruccoli, Matthew J. *Some Sort of Epic Grandeur: The Life of F. Scott Fitzgerald*. New York: Carroll & Graf Publishers, 1993.
———. *F. Scott Fitzgerald: A Life in Letters*. New York: Touchstone/ Simon & Schuster Inc., 1994.
Canfield, Mary Grace. *The Valley of the Kedron*. South Woodstock, Vt.: Kedron Associates, 1940.
Jones, Lieutenant General William K. *A Brief History of the 6th Marines*. Washington, DC: History and Museums Division Headquarters, 1987.
Klehr, Harvey, John Earl Haynes, and Kyrill M. Anderson. *The Soviet World of American Communism*. New Haven: Yale University Press, 1998.
Keuhl, John, and Jackson Bryer, eds. *Dear Scott/Dear Max: The Fitzgerald-Perkins Correspondence*. New York: Charles Scribner's Sons, 1971.
Simmons, Edwin Howard. Introduction to *Through the Wheat* by Thomas Boyd. Lincoln, Nebr.: Bison Books/ University of Nebraska Press, 2000.
Stallings, Lawrence. *The Doughboys*. New York: Harper and Row, 1963.
Van Every, Dale. *The A.E.F. in Battle*. New York: Appleton and Company, 1928.
Wilson, Edmund, ed. *F. Scott Fitzgerald: The Crack-Up*. New York: New Directions Publishing, 1993.

Index